Anonymous

Harbor Of Refuge Somerset

Anonymous

Harbor Of Refuge Somerset

ISBN/EAN: 9783744646864

Printed in Europe, USA, Canada, Australia, Japan

Cover: Foto ©Andreas Hilbeck / pixelio.de

More available books at **www.hansebooks.com**

1874.

QUEENSLAND.

MANAGEMENT OF HARBOR OF REFUGE AT SOMERSET.

REPORT.

THE BOARD appointed to examine and report upon all matters and things connected with certain statements circulated in the public papers respecting the management of the Harbor of Refuge, at Somerset, and the part alleged to have been taken by Mr. Frank Jardine, Police Magistrate at Somerset, in the pearl fisheries, regret to have to state that they have experienced great difficulty in getting evidence bearing on the subject under inquiry.

They inserted advertisements in the public papers calling upon all persons who might be able to give information to come forward; they also procured the names and addresses of several such persons, said to be in or near Brisbane, and caused written notices to be forwarded to them, and, having afterwards heard that some were unwilling to attend unless their expenses were paid, they caused further notices to be issued to them stating that all reasonable expenses would be defrayed by the Board.

The list of witnesses invited, distinguishing those who attended from those who did not attend, is appended.

The Board, however, having carefully considered such evidence (documentary and otherwise) as they have been enabled to obtain, have to report :—

1. That the "regular legal papers" carried by certain boats, referred to in Captain Moresby's Report to Commodore Stirling, were not pearl fishing licenses, but the ordinary license required by section 91 of "*The Customs Regulation Act*" to be taken out by all boats, however employed. [*Vide copy of "Vampire's" license —Separate Appendix* C.] With regard to the ownership of these boats, Mr. Jardine states that with the exception of the "Vampire," which was principally employed in the Government service in the absence of any suitable Government boat, and which was never engaged pearl fishing, they are solely owned, and that the licenses were taken out, by his brother, Mr. Charles Jardine. No evidence has been produced before the Board that can be held to invalidate this statement.

2. That Mr. Cockerill, who admits himself to be the author of the letters, and to have given the principal part of the information upon which the articles which have appeared in the public papers with reference to the settlement at Somerset were based, attended the Board, and made his statements at great length, and, as will be seen, brought many charges against Mr. Jardine. These charges were denied by Mr. Jardine, who declared his letter, addressed to the Colonial Secretary, dated 29th November, 1873 (hereto appended), to contain a true and correct statement of the occurrences therein referred to, and requested that it might be recorded as evidence.

The

The most serious charge, viz., that of employing the police pearl fishing on his own private account, the Board consider to be fully disproved by the sworn testimony of coxswain E. L. Brown (the person from whom Mr. Cockerill says he chiefly obtained his information), and other constables, taken before C. E. Beddome, Esquire, Police Magistrate, Somerset, and Lieutenant Frederick J. Rendell, R.N. The only apparent exception to this is the case of Johnny Murray, which seems to be satisfactorily explained in Mr. Jardine's letter to the Colonial Secretary, of the 29th November.

No corroborative evidence has been produced in support of the other charges; while that of the witnesses McArthur and Green, so far as it refers to them, appears rather to refute than to support them.

3. That there are two points in Mr. Cockerill's evidence to which the Board would draw especial attention—viz., where he states [*vide evidence, 22nd December, questions* 83 *et seq.*] that he knows a gentleman who can give full information regarding one of the charges; and, again [*vide evidence, 29th December*], where he states that he was offered £200 to withhold his evidence in this matter;—in both cases refusing to give the names of the persons referred to. Under these circumstances the Board cannot attach any weight whatever to such statements, but consider that they tend, if anything, to affect the credibility of the remainder of his evidence.

4. Captain Dring complains that his boats were debarred from working, owing to no licenses having been granted for them. There is no evidence to prove that application was ever made to Mr. Jardine for such licenses; and the Board are of opinion that section 91 of "*The Customs Regulation Act*" quite justified Mr. Jardine in requiring that they should be taken out prior to the boats being employed.

5. To conclude, the Board consider that none of the charges against Mr. Jardine have been proved; and that it has not been shown that the management of the settlement at Somerset, as a Harbor of Refuge, has been otherwise than efficient. But, at the same time, they cannot look upon the result of the inquiry as fully satisfactory, either to themselves or to the persons concerned; and especially to Mr. Jardine, who has had no opportunity of calling evidence to confirm his own statements, or to rebut those made against him; and they are of opinion that, should it be deemed advisable to go more closely and thoroughly into the matter than they, with the limited evidence at their command, have been able to do, it should be done by a Board or Commission having power to compel the attendance of witnesses, and to examine them upon oath; and that arrangements should be made by which the evidence of the constables and others stationed at Somerset, and especially that of Coxswain E. L. Brown, might be taken on all the matters referred to.

H. G. SIMPSON, *Chairman.*

W. L. G. DREW.

G. P. HEATH.

MINUTES OF PROCEEDINGS.

FRIDAY, 12 *DECEMBER*, 1873.

PRESENT:

The Honorable H. G. Simpson, Esquire
Captain Heath, R.N.
W. L. G. Drew, Esquire.

The Honorable H. G. Simpson, Esquire, in the Chair.

The Chairman laid upon the table a letter from the Under Colonial Secretary relative to the appointment of the Board, and enclosing certain correspondence. [*Vide Separate Appendices A and B.*]

It was resolved to insert the following advertisement in the *Courier* and *Telegraph* newspapers:—

"NOTICE.—A Board having been appointed by the Government to examine into, and report upon, all matters connected with certain statements that have been circulated in the public papers respecting the management of the Harbor of Refuge at Somerset, and certain alleged irregularities connected with the Pearl Fisheries, it is requested that all persons who may be in a position to give information on the above subjects will communicate with the undersigned as early as possible.

"H. G. SIMPSON, M.L.C., Chairman.

"Legislative Council Chambers, December 12, 1873."

It was also decided to issue invitations to the undermentioned persons, requesting them to attend for the purpose of giving evidence:—The Honorable W. H. Walsh, Esquire; Charles Frith, Esquire; Mr. J. T. Cockerill; Mr. E. W. B. Hannah.

The Board then adjourned.

MONDAY, 22 *DECEMBER*, 1873.

PRESENT:

The Honorable H. G. Simpson, Esquire
W. L. G. Drew, Esquire
Captain Heath, R.N.

The Honorable H. G. Simpson, Esquire, in the Chair.

The Minutes of the preceding meeting were read and confirmed.

A letter was read from the Honorable W. H. Walsh, Esquire, declining to attend the Board for certain reasons stated therein.

The Chairman produced and laid upon the table the log of the "Vampire."

The Honorable A. H. Palmer, Esquire, Colonial Secretary; David Dring, Esquire; and Mr. J. T. Cockerill, were examined.

The Secretary was instructed to summon the following persons to attend as witnesses:—Messrs. Tinkel, George Tyney, Burgill, John Larkins, Edward Routledge, H. M. Chester, and Turpin.

The Board adjourned until Monday, the 29th instant, at *Two* o'clock.

MONDAY, 29, *DECEMBER*, 1873.

PRESENT:

The Honorable H. G. Simpson, Esquire
Captain Heath, R.N.
W. L. G. Drew, Esquire.

The Honorable H. G. Simpson, Esquire, in the Chair.

The Minutes of the previous meeting were read and confirmed.

A letter was read from Captain Dring stating that, on application to the Custom House, full information respecting the copper referred to in his evidence could be obtained.

The Secretary produced the original entry, inwards, of the steamship "Wainui," dated the 29th of April, 1872, which was to the effect that a quantity of copper, weight unknown, was consigned to Messrs. Fenwick and Scott.

A letter from Mr. H. M. Chester, was read, stating that upon payment of his expenses, he would be prepared to attend the Board for the purpose of giving evidence.

Mr. Chester being present, the Chairman informed him that the Board had no power to allow expenses, and that if he insisted upon such payment, the matter would have to be referred to the Honorable the Colonial Secretary.

Mr.

Mr. Chester thereupon waived his claim for the present, but stated his intention to furnish it in the usual form.

Messrs. H. M. Chester, Dugald McArthur, and John F. Sloan, were examined; and Mr. J. T. Cockerill was further examined.

Mr. Jardine produced and laid before the Board the license of the "Vampire." [*Vide Separate Appendix C.*]

Mr. Cockerill stated, for the information of the Board, that certain witnesses, who had been summoned for the purpose of giving evidence, would not attend unless their expenses were paid. He also suggested that Mr. William Green, boat builder, of Kangaroo Point, should be examined.

The Chairman instructed the Secretary to issue notices to the witnesses who had been summoned and had not attended, to the effect that all reasonable loss or expense incurred by them in attending the Board, would be paid; and also to summon Mr. Green.

The Board adjourned until Wednesday, the 31st instant, at half-past *Eleven* o'clock.

WEDNESDAY, 31 *DECEMBER*, 1873.

PRESENT:

The Honorable H. G. Simpson, Esquire | W. L. G. Drew, Esquire.
Captain Heath, R.N.

The Honorable H. G. Simpson, Esquire, in the Chair.

A letter was read from Mr. E. W. B. Hannah, master of the barque "Young Australia," acknowledging receipt of summons to attend the Board, and stating that, owing to pressing business engagements, he was unable to attend.

Mr. William Wilson Green was examined; and Captain Dring was further examined.

The Board then requested Mr. Jardine to make any statement he thought necessary in reply to the charges made against him.

Mr. Jardine having concluded, the Board, after deliberation, adjourned *sine die*, to enable the Chairman to bring up his draft report.

MONDAY, 5 *JANUARY*, 1874.

PRESENT:

The Honorable H. G. Simpson, Esquire | Captain Heath, R.N.
W. L. G. Drew, Esquire

The Honorable H. G. Simpson in the Chair.

The minutes of the preceding meeting were read and confirmed.

The Chairman brought up his Draft Report, which, having been considered and amended, was agreed to, and the amended report was ordered to be printed.

The Secretary was instructed to forward to the Honorable the Colonial Secretary certain papers which were laid before the Board by Mr. Cockerill on the 22nd December, 1873, and to state that the Board had no evidence before them bearing on some of the matters to which they related, and requesting that the Honorable the Colonial Secretary would furnish any remarks upon them he might think necessary.

The Board then adjourned.

THURSDAY, 8 *JANUARY*, 1874.

The Honorable H. G. Simpson, Esquire | Captain Heath, R.N.
W. L. G. Drew, Esquire

The Honorable H. G. Simpson, Esquire, in the Chair.

The minutes of the previous meeting were read and confirmed.

The Chairman stated that in accordance with instructions the Secretary had forwarded the papers laid before the Board by Mr. Cockerill to the Honorable the Colonial Secretary, and he had since received a reply enclosing certain papers, which he produced.

Resolved, That the papers be printed and appended to the report. [*Vide Separate Appendix D.*]

The Board adjourned *sine die*.

LIST

LIST OF WITNESSES.

Witnesses who attended in answer to advertisement or without summons.

The Honorable A. H. Palmer, Esquire
Captain David Dring
Mr. Dugald McArthur
Mr. John F. Sloan.

Witnesses who attended in answer to summons.

Mr. John Thomas Cockerill
H. M. Chester, Esquire
Mr. William Wilson Green.

Witnesses summoned who did not attend.

The Honorable W. H. Walsh, Esquire
Charles Frith, Esquire
Mr. E. W. B. Hannah
Mr. Tinkel
Mr. George Tyney
Mr. Edward Routledge
Mr. John Larkins
Mr. Turpin
Mr. Burgill.

1874.

QUEENSLAND.

MANAGEMENT OF HARBOR OF REFUGE, SOMERSET.

MINUTES OF EVIDENCE

TAKEN BEFORE

A BOARD OF INQUIRY

INTO THE

MANAGEMENT OF THE HARBOR OF REFUGE AT SOMERSET.

MONDAY, 22 DECEMBER, 1873.

PRESENT.

THE HON. H. G. SIMPSON, ESQUIRE W. L. G. DREW, ESQUIRE	CAPTAIN HEATH, R.N.

THE HONORABLE H. G. SIMPSON, ESQUIRE, IN THE CHAIR.

The Honorable ARTHUR HUNTER PALMER, Esquire, Colonial Secretary, examined.

The Hon. Arthur Hunter Palmer, Esquire. 22 Dec., 1873.

1. *By the Chairman:* I think, Mr. Palmer, in place of asking you questions, I had better ask you to make any statement in this matter you think will be of use in the inquiry? Well, all I can say, Captain Simpson, is, that various rumors, as you are aware, reached the Government on the subject of alleged improprieties at Somerset. As head of the Government, and the officer in charge—principally in charge of the department at Cape York, I should have taken no notice whatever of these rumors had it not been for the report of Captain Moresby, of the "Basilisk." It would appear from the report of that gentleman that Mr. Jardine is largely engaged in pearl fishery with his own boats. [*Refers to report*]. From this report it appears that Captain Moresby was under the impression that Mr. Jardine was the owner of three large open boats and the decked boat "Vampire," and he further states that "These boats are provided with regular legal papers signed by Mr. Jardine in his capacity as a Magistrate and custom house officer. One of the boat's papers is signed by Mr. Palmer, Prime Minister of Queensland. These boats are constantly employed pearl shelling." Now, with reference to the license said to have been signed by me for pearl-shell fishing, it is an utter mistake; the only license I ever signed was a license—the usual custom-house license—for the "Vampire" to trade, and the only object I had in signing that license was to prevent her being seized by the custom-house officers at Normanton if sent with despatches for the telegraph, as it was thought highly probable would have to be done soon after the Governor's and my visit to Torres Straits, last year. The license is, I believe, before you, and if you have seen it you will be aware that it is a custom-house license. There is no license whatever required for pearl-shell fishing: I am not aware, nor is the Attorney-General aware, of any Act which renders such a license necessary. The Governor and myself were at Cape York last year, in October, and we certainly then saw no symptoms of Mr. Jardine being engaged in pearl-shell fishing. The "Vampire" had only just arrived there—was not rigged, in fact, when we were there; and I have no reason to suppose, except from this report of Captain Moresby's, that Mr. Jardine ever was employed pearl-shell fishing. Mr. Walsh has informed me, on the authority of a statement furnished by Mr. Frith, that rumors were in circulation in Sydney that Mr. Jardine and myself were partners in pearl-shell fishing. I endeavored to get Mr. Frith to substantiate, or to give the names of the parties who had said so; but without effect—I never had any reply to the letter, in fact; and I wish to contradict the statement

The Hon. Arthur Hunter Palmer, Esquire.

29 Dec., 1873.

statement in the most emphatic manner, and also to state that there has never been the slightest partnership in pearl-shell fishing, or in any other way, between Mr. Jardine and myself. The only transaction that has ever occurred having even the most remote—that would bear in any way to be spoken of in connection with this matter, arises from the fact that when Mr. Jardine was first appointed Police Magistrate at Somerset, in 1869, I gave him instructions to endeavor to foster a trade with the natives of the adjacent islands as much as possible, and for that purpose furnished him with a quantity of "trade" from the Colonial Stores. A shipment of tortoise-shell and pearl-shell was sent down by Mr. Jardine, in 1871, in payment for these stores, and he represented that he had had to engage someone to look after this trade, and that he had engaged Mr. Chester, who was his predecessor at Cape York; and also that Chester had been away in the boat for a considerable time, and he thought it was only fair that he should have one-half the proceeds for his trouble. I furnish the account sales of this tortoise-shell, sold by Dangar, Gedye, and Co. The amount received was £181 9s. 7d.; there was exchange and a stamp, 18s. 1d.; and £180 11s. 6d. was remitted to me. I put that paper in [*vide Appendix*]. Mr. Jardine had a claim against the shell—I do not understand the exact particulars of the claim, but, at all events, that was deducted from the value, and £111 5s. 9d. was paid in by me to the Bank of New South Wales, to Mr. Jardine's credit, on the 14th of August, 1871; and on the 16th of the same month, £69 5s. 9d. was paid into the Colonial Treasury, making the full amount.

2. I think you said Mr. Jardine was first appointed in 1869—I think it was 1868? I cannot be sure about that.

3. At his first appointment? He had these instructions when he was sent back in 1869 or 1870.

4. Exactly; when he was re-appointed? When he went back; he had never been removed. That is the only thing that would bear the slightest construction that we were ever engaged together in any business; and, as I show from the account sales, not a farthing of the money went into my pocket in any way. [*Looks at letter from the Hon. W. H. Walsh*]—I may say, having read the letter addressed to the Chairman of the Board by Mr. Walsh, that I have caused inquiries to be made by my own agents, in Sydney, as to the alleged rumors he informed me were in circulation there, and they can hear nothing whatever of them; and I am therefore left to suppose that they arose chiefly from the imagination of Mr. Frith.

5. Then, when you were at Somerset, you were cognizant of the fact of there being boats employed pearl-shell fishing from the settlement? No; and I do not believe there were. I knew that Mr. Jardine had a boat knocking about the Straits trading; but I never knew, and never heard, that he had a boat engaged in pearl-shell fishing.

6. Boats, not Mr. Jardine's? Oh! Yes, others; we saw a few fishing.

7. And, did you know who those boats belonged to? We saw the "Peveril," said to be full of shell, at Somerset; the "Wainui" steamer on a pearl fishing expedition; a three-masted schooner called the "Melanie" was at anchor off Wednesday Passage, with all her boats out fishing; and a fishing craft in Friday Passage. We saw her boats, and the boats of two or three other small craft I never knew the names of—the "John Knox," I think, was one.

8. You are not aware of any boats from the Settlement? None whatever.

9. I do not mean Government boats? No boats from the Settlement.

10. *By Captain Heath:* There have been reports to the effect that a document was signed by the Governor, authorising boats, or Mr. Jardine to trade—can you state whether such a document was ever signed by the Governor? I can state that the Governor never signed a document of any description, excepting the visitors' book, and I am not sure that he signed that, but I believe he did.

11. I understood you to say, that at the time you were there, you had no knowledge of any boats trading in connection with the station at Somerset? Only one boat I knew Mr. Jardine had trading in the Straits; and I may state that Mr. Jardine showed me a quantity of copper which his boat had picked up, and he offered it to me for the Queensland Government. I asked him was it picked up by the Government boat, and he said not, by his own. I refused to have anything to do with it, as I could not see what claim the Queensland Government had to it in any way.

12. *By Mr. Jardine:* Do you remember what quantity of copper there was said to be? About four tons, you told me.

13. *By Captain Heath:* Did you know at the time that Mr. Jardine's brother had boats trading in the Straits at that time? No, I do not believe he had. Mr. Jardine's brother was living with him, and doing a great deal of work without any pay. He was out after cattle nearly the whole time we were there. He tried to get some fat calves for us, and got them. Mr. Jardine's brother has never had any pay from the Government. This letter (*Telegraph*, July 28, 1873,) is contradicted in every respect by the affidavits of the men. It is no use for me to contradict it. It can easily be ascertained at the Treasury that no pay has been given to Charles Jardine, although I am quite aware that he has done Government work.

14. *By the Chairman:* Can you tell us the date of your visit to Somerset? September and October, last year.

15. Last year? In September and the beginning of October. We were back here in October.

16. *By Mr. Drew:* I think you said, Mr. Palmer, that no official report had ever reached you except that of Captain Moresby? None. I have read Mr. Cockerill's letter, and certainly there is not a word of truth in it; certainly, as far as I am concerned. I never read the letter until now.

APPENDIX.

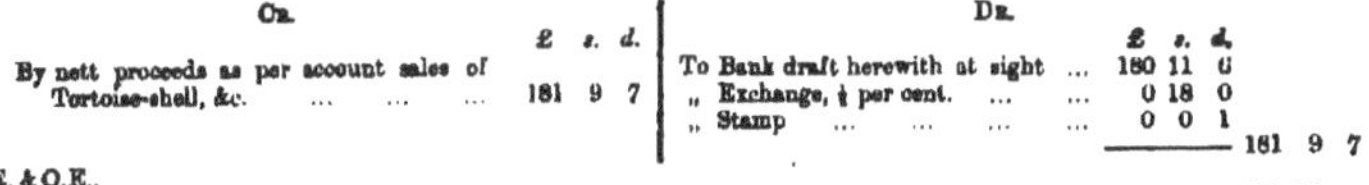

Cr.	£	s.	d.	Dr.	£	s.	d.	£	s.	d.
By nett proceeds as per account sales of Tortoise-shell, &c.	181	9	7	To Bank draft herewith at sight ...	180	11	6			
				,, Exchange, ½ per cent.	0	18	0			
				,, Stamp	0	0	1			
								181	9	7

E. & O.E.,

DANGAR, GEDYE, AND CO.

Sydney, 28th July, 1873.

Mr.

The Hon. Arthur Hunter Palmer, Esquire. 22 Dec., 1873.

Mr. Jardine puts in the following paper as evidence.

New Zealand Insurance Company,
Brisbane, 22nd December, 1873.

MY DEAR JARDINE,

With reference to the pearl-shell that was obtained while I was at Somerset, the arrangement was that I was to get half the proceeds. The shell was consigned to the Colonial Secretary, and I received, in due course, through you, a cheque for my share—about £90 or £95, as near as I can recollect; the remainder was, I believe, paid into the consolidated revenue.

Yours, &c.,
HENRY M. CHESTER.

F. Jardine, Esquire.

Captain DAVID DRING called in, and examined.

Capt. David Dring. 22 Dec., 1873.

1. *By the Chairman:* You are aware, Captain Dring, that this Board is appointed for the purpose of inquiring into matters—the truth, or otherwise, of reports that have been circulated with reference to the management of the Harbor of Refuge at Somerset, and more especially with regard to the pearl fisheries in the neighborhood? Yes, sir.

2. I received your note some little time ago, and I believe you got the answer requesting you to attend? Yes.

3. Well, we shall now be very glad to hear anything you can tell us bearing on the subject. Your name is, I believe, David Dring? David Dring.

4. What is your occupation?—Marine Surveyor? Marine Surveyor. What I have to complain of against Mr. Jardine was—I sent up boats, for the purpose of getting pearl-shell, to a person named Brown, who was his coxswain, the coxswain having written down to me that he intended to leave the service in March last; the boats had hardly got up, when Brown sent down word that Mr. Jardine would not permit them to work without a license; the consequence was they have been lying idle ever since; in looking over the Act, the Act appears to me not to require——

5. Which Act? The Act which is called the Kidnapping Act.

6. I think, perhaps, before going further, I may point out that licenses are not required at all in any degree as pearl fishing licenses; it is under "*The Customs Act*" which requires trading licenses? Well, I did not go to trade, and as it is a free port——

7. Still, "*The Customs Act*" is in force there the same as in any other port. I think you had better complete your statement, please, then we can come to that question. Have you any further complaint beyond the refusal of the license, or, rather, the refusal to allow them to trade? He stopped the boats from working, and they have been lying there ever since. When Mr. Palmer returned from Sydney, I called on him, and he said there was no occasion for any license, and he said "to end all bother, I will send up word to Mr. Jardine to grant licenses, and also make him shipping master that he may ship crews." That was a great point with me—that he should be able to ship crews. Since then, Mr. Palmer has carried that out by allowing the "Black Hawk" to go without a license, and giving the master a letter to say that no license was necessary to be issued for the purpose of pearl fishing. I went entirely by this Act, "*The Kidnapping Act,*" which says that, with regard to the crew, no license is required. This is the last Act; it is a Home Act, and it is presumed it repeals all other Acts in that respect. It distinctly states, as regards the crew, no license is required; consequently I never sent any. Then the provisions had to be sold there, and bills were taken on the South Australian Government, and paid over to me, which never could have been for the provisions sold there, because these bills were dated in January, and the provisions were sold in March; there must have been some wrong work there; they amounted, altogether, to £111 15s. 10d., they were all dishonored by the South Australian Government; I did not get them until September; these bills certainly were never taken for these provisions that were sold there; how it happened I do not know, but it is so.

8. *By Mr. Drew:* The bills were all dishonored? Yes, and I did not get them paid until September.

9. They were eventually paid? Yes, they were, but not before I had twice written to the Governor in Council.

10. Were they orders on the Government? Yes, orders on Mr. Todd, the Superintendent of Telegraphs; that is all that concerns myself; but as regards my being a Surveyor for Lloyds, again I have been informed that about 30 tons of copper came from Somerset, which, I believe, was transhipped here; it appears there was something very dark about it from beginning to end; I cannot inform the underwriters, and I cannot get at the bottom of it in any way, and it is my duty to inform them; therefore I want to get, if possible, at the bottom of that; it came down in an extraordinary way, and was transhipped here; since then I have heard payment was stopped in respect of it, by a Sydney house; it is my duty to get to the bottom of this in some way.

11. What payment was stopped? For this copper.

12. *By the Chairman:* The insurance? No, for the copper itself; it was sent home and orders were sent to the parties, by whose ships it went, not to hand over the proceeds. This has been a great loss to me; these boats lying idle all the time, and, up to this time, and as far as the Act goes, I cannot see any reason why Mr. Jardine should have stopped it, because, certainly, there is no license required; I was not going to trade with boats, and even if I was, it is a free port.

13. *By Captain Heath:* Are you not rather confusing the fact of licenses not being required under "*The Kidnapping Act,*" and the fact of licenses being required under "*The Customs Act?*" No, I perfectly understood it was required under "*The Custom House Act,*" provided you are not in a free port, but being in a free port you do not require it.

14. Are you aware that the port of Somerset only extends some five miles? No, I do not know to what extent it extends; but it does not signify; there is no place where you can smuggle within—say, 200 miles; you have either to go down to the Gulf, or go along the coast.

15. Are you not aware that any custom house officer—a sub-collector of customs—has power by law to act as shipping master where no shipping master is appointed? But if there is no sub-collector of customs?

16. Mr. Jardine is Sub-Collector of Customs? He was appointed at the same time he was appointed Shipping Master by the Colonial Secretary.

17. By

Capt. David Dring.

22 Dec., 1873.

17. *By Mr. Drew:* With regard to the remittance sent to you, who sold the provisions? Mr. Brown.
18. Your agent? Yes.
19. And he forwarded the money? He did.
20. Then, in what respect does that affect the management of Somerset, if your own agent transacted the business? I want to know where he got these bills from;—he did not take them for the provisions, I am sure; and he is not a man who has got money himself.
21. How were your boats manned for which you applied for a license? They were not manned at all; they would not allow them to work.
22. Who were intended to man them—to navigate them? Anyone we could get.
23. Do you not know that your letter, upon which the Attorney-General based his opinion, said that they were to be manned and navigated by Polynesians? No; nor yet to the Colonial Secretary;—I do not presume we could get them; I presumed we could get men from Darnley Island, or some natives about the place.
24. *By Mr. Jardine:* When did this copper come down? I should not like to tell you, speaking from memory; I remember very well bringing down the transhipping order to Webb, the tide-waiter at Lytton.
25. When? I do not like to tell you from memory; I remember it being on board one of Harris' ships.
26. What ships brought it down? That I cannot tell you, but I will very soon find out for you.
27. *By the Chairman:* Can you tell us approximately—within a month or so—as to the time the copper you speak of was transhipped? I will get it.
28. Will you send it us, to-morrow? Yes; I will—the ship, name, and everything; I will get it from the Custom House.
29. *By Mr. Jardine:* Was it shipped by me? I do not know.
30. Was it carried from Somerset? I believe it was; I was told it was not in your name.

JOHN THOMAS COCKERILL called in and examined.

Mr. J. T. Cockerill.

22 Dec., 1873.

1. *By the Chairman:* Your name is? John Thomas Cockerill.
2. What is your occupation at present? At present, I suppose, I am a collector; I am a master mariner.
3. I hold in my hand here two communications to the *Telegraph* newspaper, on the 28th of July, and the 9th of August, the second of which is signed "J. T. Cockerill." Are these statements made by you? These are statements made by me, and part of another dated the 9th of August relative—part of that leading article [*pointing to article, Telegraph, August 9th*, 1873] referring to the £500 Mr. Jardine received from the Government for doing nothing, and likewise £470 for the vessel to take him there.
4. Then, I suppose, it is no use going through all this again; do you state now, before the Board, that these statements are correct? These statements are correct.
5. Have you anything further you wish to add to them? Relative to the conduct and the affairs of Cape York generally?
6. A great number of things, I find. With regard to the pearl-fishery—that appears to be the main thing, and there is another complaint about the prices of stores? Yes, and condemned stores.
7. Very likely; anything of that sort; if you have any statements to add you had better make them at once, please. You had better take one at a time—take the pearl-fishing first, if you like? Well, as stated there, I state that Mr. Jardine has been in the habit of pearl-fishing, without a doubt, at the public expense.
8. *By Mr. Drew:* Mr. Frank Jardine? Yes, Mr. Frank Jardine; that persons belonging to the police department are nearly always, or Brown especially—of course Brown owns boats as well, and deals in pearl-shell the same as Mr. Jardine; that the wood required for these boats, is got by the Government troopers, is brought in the Government boats, and with the Government horse and dray; that water in the same manner and provisions; that when the boats arrive they are hauled up with Government men who are there, as well as white police—they all assist stripping the boats, cleaning them, painting them —of course, whether the paint and all those things belong to the Government, I am not prepared to say; all that I know is the Government stores go in there and they come out for the painting of the boats, and I am credibly informed by the men that it is Government property.
9. By what men? By the men; by the police; that the whole that they use, rope and everything else, is the property of the Government.
10. *By the Chairman:* Can you give the names of the men who made these statements? No one being expected here——
11. Can you give the names of the men who made these statements? Blunt, in particular, and Tinkel—no, that is not the name—two shipwrecked seamen belonging to the "Crown," brig; they stated to me—in fact they wished me to give the information—that they had not done one day's work for the Queensland Government since they had been there; that they had been totally, and wholly, and solely employed with, and by, Mr. Jardine pearl-fishing, and, to the best of my knowledge, they spoke the truth.
12. You do not know the names of these two men? Yes, I will give them in a minute; one is pretty well satisfied, but the other is not satisfied; one, Burgill, is in town; the other, I believe, walked off; he showed me a roll of notes and walked off.
13. Do you know the man's address in town? No; the only information I have, is that he was living with some woman, Mrs. Turner.
14. That is George Tyney: he gives his name here as George Tyney? I do not know.
15. That is the name your son gave him; I suppose that is the man; perhaps he has half-a-dozen names? I do not know it from the man himself; I stated I was not particular; I do not know particularly the names, I knew so little of the men, but I knew they were two shipwrecked seamen of the "Crown"; I asked another party who knew, perhaps, as well as myself, and he told me it was Burgill.
16. *By Mr. Drew:* It is the name you have a doubt about, but the men did communicate what you are now stating? Yes: That the work, as regards rigging the boats, making sails, hauling them up, painting them—although any fancy work—the man that paints the fancy work is always Blunt, he does the fancy work, the others do the coarser work; ribbons, and that, are done by him; the pearl-shell, when it arrives, is conveyed up to Mr. Jardine's private residence on the Government dray by the native troopers, with the assistance of some of the Murray Islanders; that the Government bullocks are in some instances wholly eaten by these men, both black and white; and I call your attention to one instance—I think one will do——

17. By

Mr. J. T. Cockerill.

22 Dec., 1873.

17. *By the Chairman:* You state one particular instance? Yes; on the 24th of December, I had one of my men, who was so weak from having no meat for eight or nine months——

18. *By Mr. Drew:* December, 1872? This year; no, of course 1872; he was removed to the shade, of course it was through weakness; I applied to Mr. Jardine to be allowed some beef to make soup for Christmas Day, and he told me he would see about it; I went up and saw him shoot the bullock, and I afterwards saw the four quarters, the head, the four legs, and tail, pass my door and go on board the "Vampire," Brown, master; I then said to Brown "Why don't they give you the tongue in with it?" I said "They ought to let the tail go with the hide"; Brown said, "No, the tongue is kept for Mr. Jardine." At night I went down to see if they were actually going to feed off the meat, and I found they were busily engaged cooking their supper, both blacks and whites, about fifty-two; of course all expectation was gone of my having any; however, on Sunday—at least, on Christmas Day—a tin of meat was sent down to Routledge, the man who laid on the sand from weakness; a tin of mutton —preserved mutton; I saw Mr. Jardine, and he said "I cannot spare it, I want it for my niggers."

19. *By the Chairman:* Spare what? The beef; he could not spare any beef. I have had frequent communications with Brown and others as to whether they were satisfied with their being taken from their duties; they said no, they were not, but they said it could not be altered, "as the Court was held in hell and the devil presided." That is what was their own words—it was no use making any complaint. I give it to you word for word as I heard it. Brown said—notwithstanding what he says since—I pity the man—Brown says "If I was placed upon my oath about this matter, see what a position I should stand in; here am I receiving not less than five pays from the Government, and never do a day's work for them. I receive pay as postmaster; I receive pay as storekeeper; I receive pay as coxswain; I receive pay as policeman; and I receive the Government rations and clothes, and medicine, and everything else, and I do no duty for them." "And then the pearl-fishing business," he says, "is killing me by inches;" and he said, if it had not been for the black woman he was allowed to take with him, he would not have stopped another day; that was the only inducement.

20. What? The black woman he had from Cape York, he was allowed to have on board the boat.

21. *By Mr. Drew:* The Government boat, or which boat? Oh, no; neither of these are Government boats. The "Vampire" is not a Government boat.

22. *By the Chairman:* Is it the "Vampire" you are alluding to? The "Vampire" I am alluding to. At the same time, Brown spoke very seriously on the matter, because he thought it was a serious matter that all illegal acts—and I can safely say there is not a few of them—all these illegal acts are written in pencil. He showed me a handful of pencil orders he tried, if possible, to get into ink. He was told, "You have got my order, and that is sufficient for you." He tried to get Mr. Jardine to put these orders in ink, but he continued to give them in pencil, and refused; they were only certain orders mind—only orders in case of anything—because you must understand me, that transactions in Cape York, as far as I can say, and I had very good opportunity of judging and hearing, it is all fictitious—names are fictitious; the Government rations are sold in fictitious names in nine cases out of ten; and I believe cheques are in fictitious names. I do not doubt it; copper is sent down in fictitious names; pearl-shell is sent down in fictitious names—in fact, it is all fictitious. Cape York is nothing but a pearl-fishing station at the Government expense. It may be argued that it belongs to a boy who is there; I heard so.—[*The Board adjourned for one hour, and resumed at two o'clock.*]

23. I think you were about to say something about the stores? I think, perhaps, it would be as well first to inform the Board that if a man named Turpin is called he will give some useful information on both sides; and, also, a man named Larkin and Mr. Chester.

24. *By Mr. Drew:* Why Mr. Chester? Because he is the writer of the other letter, and I think it is right he should be here, particularly as I do not wish to shirk the matter.

25. *By the Chairman:* Which letter? The letter of the 9th of August, 1873.

26. Perhaps you will be good enough to point out what is Mr. Chester's, and put the letter "C" against it. [*Witness marks portion of article from the words "Just to show how much this feeling" to end of paragraph, in the manner directed.*]

26. *By the Chairman:* Now will you go on with what you were stating? I will just state two small facts; they are only very trivial in themselves, but I think the reign of terror ought not to be held over persons in this manner. One of the men, I call them Tinkles (I do not wish to give a man a nick-name, but it is one of the sailors of the "Crown"), came to me and said, "I am going to take out your 'heart thimbles.'" I said, "You do not do anything of the kind." He said, "I have Mr. Jardine's orders to do so."

27. What "heart thimbles?" Those heart thimbles placed in the rigging.

28. The rigging of your boat? The standing rigging, both from the jib-stay and the main-stay and the fore-stay. Shortly after my breakfast I came down and I found the "thimbles" had been taken out and replaced by round ones. Now round "thimbles" are not at all adapted for standing wire rigging. Of course I objected, but remonstrance was out of the question. On the passage down, these very same places drew, and nearly let my masts overboard. However, I had to heave the vessel to and replace them in the best manner I could, and I have had to get new since. The thimbles were handed to Mr. Jardine, and placed in the rigging by——

29. Into what rigging? Into the rigging of the "Vampire," by Blunt; I do not say that Mr. Jardine ever asked me, or had anything to do with this; I am speaking as far as I know of the police and who did this; I do not know what passed between them; I knew it was no use; I stood in very bad grace there.

30. Now, you have said something about condemned stores? The next thing is that I was going to leave some of my charts and books in the hands of Mr. Brown, and Mr. Jardine says, "No, if you leave them with him they will only get destroyed and dirtied." I left them with Mr. Jardine for safety; on returning I was told the captain walked down to the beach with them under his arm.

31. On returning when—two years afterwards or six months? I believe it was four days; that is what Thorngreen—I did not return, but I left for the Aroo Islands—but Thorngreen, master of a sailing vessel down there, told me that he saw the captain of one of the vessels with my charts under his arm.

32. Did he mention the name of the vessel? Yes, but I cannot think of the name; he said, "You had better see after them." I went up to Mr. Jardine and he had forgotten all about them; I called his

attention

Mr. J. T. Cockerill.

22 Dec., 1873.

attention to the fact that I could see one or two of them there in the place, and that there were those with me who could prove that they were brought there for safety.
33. There were persons who could prove at that time? Yes, Mr. Jardine said, "I never expected to see you any more and I gave them away in mistake." He said, "Here, pick what you like out of those." Now this is one of my charts I left [*chart produced*]; they were new when I left; that is one of my charts, and these [*producing several charts*] are samples I got; they were incomplete, and rags, and old, different altogether to mine; that is all I have to say; it is only merely trifling things, but I think it is scarcely right; I will first put in that [*producing paper*], if you please, it will be better than my speaking.
34. You put this in? Yes, I can write it much more clearly than I can speak it.
35. This applies to the seizure of a boat of Delargy, Dare, and Tait? Yes. [*Paper put in and marked A, vide Appendix.*] I also put these in—[*Vide Appendix B, and Separate Appendix D.*]
36. *By the Chairman:* Have you any further statement? Yes; that Mr. Jardine, in January last, told me he held an exclusive right to carry on the pearl fishing business with the boats then going out. It then came about securities; he told me that His Excellency the Governor is one of his securities, and that Mr. Palmer, Colonial Secretary, is the other security for this boat.
37. For what? For the "Vampire," pearl fishing. When the "Vampire" was hauled on shore, Blunt took the said document out and said, "What do you think of us, Cockerill, the kings of Torres Straits?" I think he mentioned something joking about the king of Torres Straits. He showed me the document and said, "You will see Mr. William Palmer's name attached to that; that is what none of them have got besides us." Larkin has read the document, I have not; but Mr. Jardine told me the document he held in his hand was the document.
38. If it will shorten matters, I may state the Board have seen the "Vampire's" license, and it was signed by Mr. Palmer.—As for it being signed by the Governor, that is another thing.—It is not worth while going into that.—It is an ordinary Custom House license, signed by Mr. Palmer? It may not be the Governor's signature. I could not say so.
39. Is there any further statement? As far as I am concerned, I am quite willing, if there is the slightest mistake, that His Excellency's name shall be taken from it, because I cannot say it was signed by him. I can only go from what was shown me.
40. *By Mr. Drew:* I think you stated that Coxswain Brown had informed you that he had been employed on private business—Mr. Jardine's private business, pearl fishing, and other matters at Cape York, and he objected to it? He did, most decidedly.
41. There was a naval court or an inquiry at Cape York before the captain of the man of war there, and I find to the question, "Have you ever been employed in any boats pearl fishing"? this Mr. Coxswain Brown says, "Never whilst in Government employ, except during my leave, when I was working on my own account."—That is his reply, and can you reconcile the two statements? No, sir, I cannot. We are all perfectly aware that he has been employed in it for two years. It is like holding a pistol to a man's head, and asking him for a loan of half-a-crown.
42. There is a further question by the court, "Have the Government boats ever been employed pearl-fishing," to which Brown answers, "No," on oath at the time? I believe not; I believe they were all private boats.
43. And Brown is one of your principal authorities for the statements you have been making? Yes, the principal part of my information has been gained from Brown.
44. At different interviews, or one? At different interviews.
45. What was the length of your stay at Cape York? Altogether, I think I was at Cape York about five months.
46. *By the Chairman:* At one time, or oftener? Two different times, about two and a-half months each, as well as I can remember.
47. *By Mr. Jardine:* I think you said, in the first part of your evidence, that Brown owns pearl fishing boats? I believe he owns two.
48. Did you see them? I am not sure that they were his at the time I saw the boats, but I have seen letters from him since, and he states the boats are his property. The "Uno" was one; I believe that was the name of one. I have seen his letters, and I only wish I could produce them here, gentlemen.
49. Further on you said that Brown was receiving pay as postmaster, storekeeper, coxswain, and policeman; do you know what pay he receives as storekeeper? He told me £20; I know this only from what I heard from him; he told me he received pay for storekeeper, £20.
50. You say that you saw orders? Yes.
51. *By the Chairman:* Do you mean sailing orders? Instructions issuing for provisions, and to fine a man a pound for coming down without his revolver; that is what I am alluding to now.
52. *By Mr. Jardine:* Were these things written in a book? They were written by you in the boat-shed, in pencil; they were not written in a book, but on a piece of paper that size [*pointing to paper*] in the boat-shed.
53. That is only one case? That is the only one I saw; I saw the others; of course I knew the writing; in reference to that, it was fining Tinkel, one of the seamen of the "Crown," a pound for coming down without his pistol.
54. That was the order I wrote in the boat-shed? That was the order; it was not carried out because Brown refused to make an entry of it, because the man had not been charged, and it was written in pencil; I heard that in conversation.
55. You say in one of these letters of yours in the paper, that my brother is receiving pay from the Government? He told me so.
56. Did any one else tell you so? Yes.
57. Who? Captain Hannah told me you told him you would have him down as passenger, and he was coming down as stockman to Cape York.
58. You remember these charts you spoke to me about. I could not find the charts at first, but you remember me giving you a bundle of charts from the top of the bookcase? You did.
59. Those charts were yours—were they not? They were; the blue ones were mine, but the coast sheets were not.

60. *By*

Mr. J. T. Cockstill.

22 Dec., 1873.

60. *By Mr. Drew:* You said you saw the beef (portion of a beast) taken for the use of the crews of private boats? The whole of it, with the exception of the tongue.
61. Was the beast the property of the Government? The beast was the property of the Government and no other.
62. Are you personally aware that it was not paid for by those who took it, or their employer? No, I cannot say; their employer was of course the Government and Mr. Jardine; Brown, Tinkel, Blunt, and those who were connected with the boat's crew were paid by the Government, and Jemmy Murray and one or two others were paid by the Government, for belonging to the boat's crew, and they had a right to eat the meat because they were the Government men.
63. You applied for a portion I think for your own crew? Yes.
64. Did you expect to pay for it? Of course I did.
65. Did you receive any? I received two pieces.
66. Did you pay for it? Indirectly. Do you wish to know how I paid for it?
67. Yes? Mr Jardine said, "You want a few little things and I want the poodle dog you have there"—a white curly poodle—"and I want some cassawary's eggs." The poodle dog and cassawary's eggs were given in consideration for the two pieces of meat I got; Mr. Jardine was kind enough to give us some milk occasionally, which was included in the transaction, I think.
68. But why, when you are not slow to see the impropriety of others taking Government property without paying for it, did you not see that you paid for what you got in a proper manner? You are alluding to the meat; I asked Mr. Jardine what was to pay, and when the Government officer said he was satisfied with the pay he received it was all right; that did not include rations; they were paid for in money.
69. *By Captain Heath:* In cash? In cash.
70. What about the dishonored cheque? I do not know.
71. Did you give a cheque? No; I know nothing of it more than you sitting there. I have called at the office about it, and they do not know anything about it.
72. You, of course, saw these boats that were there? I did.
73. Was there any name on them? Yes.
74. Owner's name? Mr. Jardine's name is on the "Vampire." Mr. Brown put it on.
75. His name, we know, is on the "Vampire's" license; but on the other boats? I am not sure whether Mr. Jardine's name is or is not attached to them. I know one of them is the "Roepuncum," and the "Restless." I do not know the names of the other two. I could get the names of the others if it is of any consequence.
76. How often were these boats at Somerset during the five months you were there? The five boats left——
77. How often were they there? They went away on the 24th of December; one, the "Vampire," was dismasted and returned; got a mast in and went away again; and by the time I left the other boats had not returned.
78. Only once at the Settlement? Only once at the Settlement. Brown was in one, because the mast was carried away of the "Vampire," and the next time he took in stores for the boats on the fishing ground on the Ormond Reefs.
79. Did you say pearl-shell has been shipped by Mr. Jardine in fictitious names? Yes.
80. Can you give any information about it? I know it from the captain of the vessel.
81. *By the Chairman:* Which vessel? In one instance the "Gleaner," Bowman, captain. Bowman told me it was strange Jardine did not ship copper in his own name.
82. *By Captain Heath:* I was speaking of pearl-shell? Yes; pearl-shell and copper both; but I am positive about him telling me it was a strange appearance not shipping the copper in his own name.
83. But can you state positively about the pearl-shell? No; it is only hearsay. I have no doubt about the pearl-shell, but there is a gentleman here has the full information.
84. *By the Chairman:* Who is that? Well, I scarcely think I am justified in compromising a member of the Government.
85. If you can tell us do so, because we are bound to get all the evidence we possibly can. We have had extreme difficulty in getting anyone? People have an objection to run their head into law without remuneration. I would not. If I did not commit myself to paper I would not have appeared, only considering having given information I had a right to be here to support it.
86. You state there is a gentleman here who can support that statement, and yet you do not give his name. It is a very difficult matter, you know, for the Board to give any weight to such evidence. I ask you once again—You state there is a gentleman here who can state that this shipment was made in a feigned name, and can prove it; do you decline giving his name to the Board? I can get the name the copper was shipped in if you like.
87. No; the name of the gentleman who can prove the name it was shipped in? I am aware he would not—it would not be wise or politic for him to do so.
88. I tell you we wish to get every information possible? He will give me the information.
89. That will not do. We do not take secondary evidence? No, I cannot. I would be very sorry to see him, and I am sure you would too.

APPENDIX A.

Somerset, Cape York,
January, 1873.

Seizure of a Boat belonging to Delargey, Dare, and Tait.

This afternoon I went with two of the police to seize a boat belonging to Delargey, Dare, and Tait. Dare and Tait were in the boat; she was schooner rigged, painted red; funny built; she was seized by order of F. L. Jardine, P.M., of Cape York. Charge: not having the name on stern—and confiscated to the Crown; the broad-arrow was put upon the masts and bows of the boat before the gear was removed. I advised Birgill (seaman of the "Crown" brig) to take an inventory of the goods; he went to Mr. Jardine to inquire; when he came back, he said all that was necessary was boat, masts and sails, chain and anchor; all other things, viz.:—5 five-gallon kegs, 1 ten-gallon keg, 1 large awning to cover the whole of the boat, 1 smaller awning, 1 new foresail (these were all quite new), mainsail, jib, &c.; a quantity of cooking utensils, and a lot of sundries; no inventory was taken of these articles;

Mr. J. T. Cockerill. 28 Dec., 1873.

articles; I helped to put them into the boat-shed. After Dare and Tait were gone to Darnley, Mr. Jardine said, "these will do for the 'Vampire,' exactly what we wanted," pointing to the articles above-mentioned. He then said "Cockerill, how do you tan your sails such a nice color?" I said with the bark of mangrove tree; I said it looks well and lasts a long time. Mr. Jardine said, "I will tan these," pointing to the awnings and foresail; he then ordered one of the troopers to get the bark, as directed by me; the two awnings and foresail were taken to Mr. Jardine's house and tanned; these were all new; I next saw them on board the "Vampire," Brown's boat; the kegs were distributed in all the boats, also the cooking gear; as Blunt put them into the boat he said "this is what we do with condemned stores of Cape York," &c. The papers in the Colonial Secretary's Office will, or ought to, show this seizure. Dare and Tait are still at Darnley and Murry.

J. T. COCKERILL.

APPENDIX B.

THE GOVERNMENT BOAT CONDEMNED, IN FEBRUARY, 1871, AT SOMERSET, CAPE YORK, BY THE OFFICER OF H.M.S.

Shortly after my arrival at Cape York, in 1871, one of the men anchored a Government boat at my stern; when the tide left, my anchor went through the boat, breaking two planks; after the police cleared it, they reported it to Mr. Jardine, who said let it alone, the man-of-war will be here in a day or two and I will get it condemned; it was condemned. After the man-of-war had gone, the boat was brought under the verandah of the Custom House, and remained there until I returned; it was then removed to the boat-house to be repaired; Captain Moresby asked me one day, while looking at my birds, why the boat was there, I said it was condemned last year, he said then it had a right to be destroyed.

J. T. COCKERILL,
Late Master of the "Naturalist," Schooner.

MONDAY, 29 DECEMBER, 1873.

PRESENT.

THE HON. H. G. SIMPSON, ESQUIRE W. L. G. DREW, ESQUIRE	CAPTAIN HEATH, R.N.

THE HONORABLE H. G. SIMPSON, ESQUIRE, IN THE CHAIR.

HENRY MAJORIBANKS CHESTER called in and examined.

H. M. Chester, Esquire. 29 Dec., 1873.

1. *By the Chairman:* Your name is? Henry Majoribanks Chester.
2. How do you describe yourself?—Have you any special profession here at present? Yes; commission agent.
3. You have been requested to attend, Mr. Chester, at the suggestion of Mr. Cockerill partly, and partly because the Board supposed, having been at Somerset in charge for some time, you might have some knowledge of the matters now under inquiry. Mr. Cockerill has stated that you wrote this statement marked in pencil here—that is to say, this portion of the leading article in the *Telegraph* of August the 9th, marked in pencil [*pointing to portion of article commencing "Just to show how much this feeling has been fostered," to end of paragraph*]? I should have been more accurate had I written it; I supplied the information upon which this is written; there are one or two inaccuracies in it.
4. Can you correct these inaccuracies?—I mean, can you give us what is correct—what ought to have been stated? It says, just about the time Mr. Jardine's leave of three months expired, Mr. Palmer became Mr. Lilley's successor;—but Mr. Palmer did not come into office until nearly twelve months afterwards—about nine months after the expiration of the three months' leave; I am not quite sure as to the exact time.
5. Is that all? That is the latter portion of it; I supplied the information upon which this is framed; of course it is all in the editor's own phraseology.
6. You were sometime in charge of the Settlement at Somerset yourself? Yes, for twelve months.
7. Up to what period were you there? About the 20th of August, 1870, I left; or rather I gave over charge.
8. You were for some time after that, I believe, in that neighborhood? Two years, nearly.
9. Do you remember when you finally left Torres Straits? In March, 1872, I think.
10. Do you know anything with reference to these statements that have been made as to pearl fishing from the station at Somerset? I know nothing further than what I heard from Mr. Cockerill, and from what I have seen in the papers; I had left the Settlement, and, consequently, can know nothing about them.
11. You had left the Settlement before these alleged irregularities took place? Yes; before they took place.
12. *By Captain Heath:* Had Mr. Charles Jardine any boats up there at that time? No; none.
13. *By Mr. Jardine:* Do you remember Captain Moresby condemning the Government boat at Somerset? Yes.
14. The old police boat? Yes.
15. Was she used after she was condemned, as far as you know? Well, we have gone out to the oyster rock in her fishing. It is not a mile outside the pass. She was rotten.
16. That was after she was condemned? She was condemned just before I came away. She was rotten long before; she was condemned several times.
17. After she was condemned by Captain Moresby? No; I am not aware she was ever used after that.
18. *By the Chairman:* There is one question more I would like to ask.—The "Basilisk" was up at Cape York before you left; what date was that, do you remember? She came up there in the latter end of February, 1872; the middle or latter end of the month; I cannot say the exact date.
19. *By Mr. Drew:* Mr. Cockerill was not at Cape York at the time you were there? Oh, yes; he was there. When he arrived I was away in the "Basilisk." He was there about a month or six weeks while I was there.
20. Did he ever complain to you of the management of the Settlement? No; he never did.

DUGALD

Dugald McArthur, Esquire.

29 Dec., 1873.

DUGALD MCARTHUR called in and examined.

1. *By the Chairman:* You are aware of the purpose for which the Board is sitting, Mr. McArthur? Yes; I believe I have seen something about it in print.
2. You are aware it is with regard to the management of the Settlement at Cape York? Yes.
3. The Board have been informed that you wish to be examined upon the subject—is that so? Yes.
4. We are ready to hear any statement you wish to make, if you will be kind enough to make a statement? The statement I have to make is respecting this man who is accusing Mr. Jardine.
5. *By Captain Heath:* What man?—Mr. Cockerill, do you mean? This Mr. Cockerill; I came to Cape York in the "May Queen," as mate of her, from Normanton, on the 23rd of December last year.
6. *By the Chairman:* On the 23rd of December, 1872, you came to Cape York in the "May Queen"? Yes; about three and a-half hours afterwards Captain Cockerill arrived at Cape York in a little bit of a schooner.
7. Is that what is called the "Naturalist"? Yes; I believe she was called the "Naturalist"; I had never seen the man before, but I believe he was acquainted with Captain Thomas, of the "May Queen," in Sydney; he came to anchor under the stern of the "May Queen," just about as far as you could throw a biscuit on board; Captain Thomas sang out to him—I cannot say whether it was Mr. Cockerill sang out to Captain Thomas or Captain Thomas sang out to him first, but he came on board and wanted to know if there was any medicine on board; he told us a man died down at the Aroo Islands, and that his own son was lying sick on board; we gave him some medicine, and Mr. Jardine here, when he found out there was a sick man on board, and that Cockerill was going to proceed to Sydney next day, he would not allow him to proceed with a sick man on board, with fever, and he gave him medicine.
8. On board the "Naturalist"? Yes.
9. Did he ask you for medicine? He asked Captain Thomas, and Captain Thomas gave him some we had from Normanton; I gave him a drop of laudanum, and a package of salts and senna.
10. We do not quite understand what Mr. Jardine had to do with this matter? Well, I have seen slips of paper sent down there from Brisbane or Sydney, I do not know which, stating that Mr. Jardine was having shipwrecked crews on shore putting fences up; now, I have been down there for the last eight months, and I have been there before, and I have never seen anyone working at fences.
11. What slips? Slips of printing taken out of the paper and sent down there.
12. Did Cockerill state to you that this was the case? No; my own eyes told me, because I can read; I seen it in the papers, and I call it right-down falsehood.
13. *By Mr. Drew:* What you saw in the papers you call right-down falsehood? Yes.
14. *By the Chairman:* You say it is not true? No.
15. Is this the statement you refer to—"On the shipwrecked mariners' topic nothing was ever said by me, but I know they are compelled to work, fencing, &c., or they get only sufficient rations to keep them alive"? No, it is not; it is not the statement that I read.
16. I cannot see the exact charge you refer to, but do I understand you state that these charges with regard to shipwrecked mariners having been forced to work at fencing and other things of that sort are not true? Yes; there is not as much as a particle of truth in all of them as far as my experience of the time I have been down there; I have been there twice before, and I have been eight months in the place with Mr. Jardine, and I could see if there was.
17. How long were you at Somerset or in the neighborhood;—in Torres Straits altogether? I have been twice in Torres Straits.
18. How long have you been connected with the Settlement at Somerset? I have been connected with it—I called there twice in the "May Queen," going up and coming down; we discharged six tanks there going up to Normanton.
19. You took up the "Lizzie Jardine"? Yes.
20. You were employed there for some time? Yes.
21. For how long can you say, altogether? Well, I left here at ten o'clock on the 5th of May.
22. And when did you leave Somerset last? I left in November.
23. During that time you were a good deal at the Settlement, I suppose? Well, yes.
24. Frequently? Frequently.
25. Had you any opportunity, or were you in the habit of hearing anything from the police constables with regard to the work of the station?—Had you any conversation with them? I had very little conversation with them, because ——
26. Did you ever hear any complaints about the manner in which they were treated or worked? I did not.
27. Have you anything further you wish to state on your own account? I can say that the statements made in the papers that were sent down there, whatever office they were printed in, or whoever was the instigation of printing them, they were untrue; there is no man who can go to the station and manage it better than Mr. Jardine, according to my experience.
28. You say these statements were untrue? They were malicious in their statements against Mr. Jardine.
29. Do I understand that in your opinion Mr. Jardine managed the station satisfactorily? Yes.
30. *By Captain Heath:* You said you were at the station on the 24th of December? Yes; on the 24th of December I left.
31. Last year? Yes.
32. The "Naturalist" was there then? Yes.
33. Did you get any meat from the station on board the "May Queen" on that day? Yes, we did, I believe.
34. Do you know how much? Well, I cannot say.
35. A quarter or two quarters? We got as much fresh meat from the station as would refresh us.
36. Were you on shore that day at the station? Not that day; we left that day; we were on shore on the 23rd for water.
37. Were there any fishing boats at the Settlement at that time? There were only two or three at that time.
38. What boats were they? Well, I cannot say now, sir; I cannot tell the names now.

39. Whose

Dugald McArthur, Esquire. 29 Dec., 1873.

39. Whose boats were they? There was that barque that was taken up.
40. The "Crishna"? No; the "Woodbine," I think; she was down at what they call Mud Bay when we passed her.
41. *By the Chairman:* These were her boats? She was getting her sails bent.
42. *By Captain Heath:* I asked you what boats were at the Settlement that day; what fishing boats? There were no fishing boats there at all; not that I recollect.
43. At the Settlement? No, except Cockerill's. When we were going down a boat of Delargy's was there.
44. Were there any fishing boats on the beach at the Settlement? No, there were no fishing boats.
45. There were only the Government boats at the Settlement; is that what you mean? That is all.
46. If there had been any other boats on the beach at the Settlement would you have known it? Oh, yes; I would have seen them.
47. Are you aware that Mr. Jardine's brother has boats at the station, or boats fishing in the Straits? Yes, I am aware he has boats; I know he has got boats there.
48. Have you seen these boats at the station? Yes.
49. How often were they at the station? Oh, pretty often; not very often.
50. You know Brown, coxswain of the police boat? Yes.
51. Has he any boats engaged pearl fishing? Not to my knowledge.
52. Have you ever heard that he had? I did.
53. Do you know the names of the boats? I could not say, sir.
54. From your knowledge of what took place at the station, can you state whether Government men are employed in these fishing boats of Mr. Charles Jardine? No.
55. Are you sure since you have been at the station that has not been the case? Oh, no; never once since I have been there.
56. Has Mr. Jardine, to your knowledge, taken any active part in pearl fishing—Mr. Frank Jardine? No, never to my knowledge.
57. *By Mr. Drew:* You spoke of a sick man on board the "Naturalist"? Yes.
58. Mr. Cockerill, on examination, says Mr. Jardine refused to allow this sick man any portion of fresh beef that was there, though he stood sadly in need of it. Is that the case? That is what I find must be false, for during the time I have been down there I have seen Mr. Jardine taking men and keeping them in his own house.
59. Sick men? Yes, sick men. There was Captain McAusland, who was there four days before I came up, and he was kept by Mr. Jardine in his own private place.
60. Do I understand you to say Mr. Jardine gave this sick man medicine, his own medicine? Yes; he would not allow Cockerill to proceed to sea until such time as he could try and do what he could for him, giving him medicine and refreshments as far as the station could afford it.
61. Do you know anything about the Government stores at Somerset?—Had you anything to do with them? No, I had nothing to do with the Government stores.
62. Did you ever hear of any Government stores, or do you know of any Government stores ever having been used in the fishing-boats? No, not that I know of.
63. You never heard of it? No, sir; except blankets that were given out.
64. *By the Chairman:* To whom? To the native blacks.
65. *By Mr. Jardine:* Do you think if there had been a lot of natives on the beach on the 24th of December, you would have seen them sleeping there? No; I could see them.
66. *By the Chairman:* You would have seen them if they were there? Yes.
67. Did you see them? No.
68. *By Captain Heath:* You were not on shore on the 24th? No; on the 23rd.
69. *By Mr. Jardine:* Did you see natives there on the 23rd? No.

John Thomas Cockerill recalled and examined.

Mr. J. T. Cockerill. 29 Dec., 1873.

1. *By the Chairman:* Mr. Cockerill, we have thought it necessary to ask you to appear again, in consequence of a report that has come to the ears of the Board since you were last examined. Certain members of the Board have heard it stated positively that you have publicly stated that you have been offered £200 by an influential person in Brisbane, not to give evidence in this case. Is that true or not? Well, I would not say distinctly it was true, in this way. I was offered £100. The party said—"Of course you know I have no interest in this matter, one way or another; I am simply acting as a solicitor; will you take £100, and have nothing more to do with this affair?" I stood some time and considered, and I said—"Would you make it £200?" Those are exactly the words. He said—"Yes; I have no doubt I can make it two." Well, I said—"Will you give me a cheque for the amount?" He said—"No; I will give you the money." I said—"What security have you got to offer me in the event of my taking it?" Of course, he saw the question perfectly well; he could offer me no security. I said—"You know perfectly well the consequence of a thing of this sort, and it is impossible for me to take it." He then said—"Would a good Government situation be of service to you; I can get it." I said—"A good Government situation would be of no service to me; I would not keep it a week; I should want you to guarantee I could keep it." He then said—"The conversation must end here." He said—"Of course, you cannot mention my name in the matter, because if you did I should be compelled to deny it, and then I should enter an action against you." I said—"I am aware of it—perfectly well aware of it."
2. That is all that occurred? That is all that occurred.
3. The next question I have to put to you is—Will you state to the Board the name of the person who made you this offer? No; I cannot. It is highly actionable. I have had the opinion of a barrister upon it, and he said—"If you mention the name you are actionable; nothing can save you."
4. *By Mr. Drew:* Did this solicitor, I think you stated him to be, intimate to you that he was authorised to act for anyone? He said he was authorised to act.
5. Authorised by whom? He did not tell me; he did not mention anyone, because he might be actionable himself.
6. *By the Chairman:* I shall, as a matter of form, put the question to you again:—Do the Board clearly understand you will not give the name of the gentleman?—Of course, we have nothing to do with your reasons? Yes, I do. The reasons are, I would be highly actionable. John

JOHN F. SLOAN called in and examined.

Mr. J. F. Sloan. 29 Dec., 1873.

1. *By the Chairman:* Your name, please; your christian name? John F. Sloan.
2. You are a clerk in the Treasury, I think? Yes.
3. *By Mr. Drew:* You hand in some copies of correspondence relative to Captain Dring's application for a license. A letter of application for a license dated February, 1873, and the Attorney-General's opinion thereon? Yes [*producing papers. Vide Appendix*].
4. Are those correct copies? Yes, these are correct copies.

APPENDIX.

Kangaroo Point, Brisbane,
Queensland, 11th February, 1873.

SIR,

I have the honor to inform you that I own four open whale boats engaged in the pearl fishery near Somerset, Cape York.

I applied to the Hon. W. Thornton, Collector of Customs, for licenses for them, but he informed me that it was out of his department.

I am at a loss to know whom I should apply to,

May I take the liberty to suggest that I think F. L. Jardine, Esq., P.M., at Cape York, might grant the licenses and act as Shipping Master for the crews, which are composed of Kanakas, New Guinea negroes, Malays, and natives of the colony. These people are the best divers, and are therefore employed.

If these people were also paid off at the end of their engagements before Mr. Jardine, it would put an end to a great deal of bad report.

It will be necessary to send soon, to save the boats being seized by H.M.S. "Basilisk," and thus crushing a trade which may prove serviceable to Queensland.

I have, &c.,
DAVID DRING.

The Honorable J. P. Bell, Treasurer, &c., &c.

Copy of Memorandum by the Honorable the Attorney-General upon Mr. Dring's Application.

If a fishing license is meant—none is required. If a license under "*The Kidnapping Act*," there is no power to authorise Mr. Jardine to issue them.

The appointment of Mr. Jardine as Shipping Master, to enter these men as crews of Captain Dring's boats, might take them out of the provisions of "*The Kidnapping Act*," but they cannot be brought before Mr. Jardine for the purpose without infringing our "*Polynesian Laborers Act*," section 1 of which Act forbids the introduction of any Polynesian laborers into the colony, except in accordance with the regulations contained in the Act.

It would be well to appoint Mr. Jardine Shipping Master, and give him instructions to supervise, as far as possible, the engagement and payment of aboriginal natives, and of other colored laborers, not Polynesians, employed in the pearl-shell fishery.

(Initialed) J.B.
A.G.

Memorandum recommending Mr. Jardine's appointment as Shipping Master, &c., at Somerset, for the purpose of enabling him to grant licenses to boats, &c.

Recommended that Mr. F. L. Jardine be appointed Shipping Master at Somerset, and Custom House Officer at Port Albany, for the purpose of enabling him to grant licenses to boats for trading purposes, under the 91st and 92nd sections of "*The Customs Act*" (9 Victoria, No. 15).

Further, that Mr. Jardine be instructed to supervise, as far as he possibly can, the payment of the men employed in pearl-shell fishery in the neighborhood of Cape York, and that he be given clearly to understand that the powers conferred upon him do not enable him to grant licenses for, or by any other means to authorise the employment of Polynesians; their employment being regulated by "*The Polynesian Laborers Act of* 1867," and by "*The Kidnapping Act of* 1872."

The Board adjourned until half-past Eleven o'clock a.m., on Wednesday.

WEDNESDAY, 31 *DECEMBER*, 1873.

PRESENT.

THE HON. H. G. SIMPSON, ESQUIRE | W. L. G. DREW, ESQUIRE.
CAPTAIN HEATH, R.N.

THE HONORABLE H. G. SIMPSON, ESQUIRE, IN THE CHAIR.

WILLIAM WILSON GREEN called in and examined.

1. *By the Chairman:* What is your christian name? William Wilson.
2. Your occupation? Boat builder.
3. The Board have requested your attendance, Mr. Green, in consequence of it having been stated by Mr. Cockerill that you could give some evidence upon the matters now under the notice of the Board, namely, Mr. Jardine's connection with the pearl fisheries up at Somerset, and also the general management of the station. Can you give us any information upon those points? I had left there previous to the pearl fishing commencing. What pearls were got before I left were got by Mr. Chester.

Mr. W. W. Green. 31 Dec., 1873.

4. During the time you were at Cape York Mr. Chester was the only person you knew of who was employed pearl fishing? Yes.
5. Were you aware that Mr. Chester was employed by the Government for that purpose? I understood so.
6. As the Board has been appointed to inquire into all matters connected with the management of the station at Somerset, can you give us any information, or state your opinion as to the manner in which it was managed by Mr. Jardine during the time you were there? I always considered it was managed as satisfactorily as it was possible to do so; I never saw anything wrong.

7. It

Mr. W. W. Green.

31 Dec., 1873.

7. It has been stated in the public papers that men who could have given evidence condemnatory of Mr. Jardine's management of the station, were afraid to do so for fear of being ill-treated while they were on the spot. Is it your opinion that anything of the sort was the case? No; I never heard a man make such a complaint.

8. From your knowledge of the manner in which the station was conducted while you were there, are you of opinion that if such a complaint were made it would be likely to be well-founded? No; I do not think it would be well-founded at all. The men who were there when I was up would go back now if they had the chance. There are two or three of them I know would.

9. *By Mr. Drew:* How long were you at Cape York? From the 4th of April, 1870, to the last day in March, 1871.

10. Twelve months? Yes.

11. The management during that time appeared to you to be good? Yes; I never saw any cause for complaint at all.

12. *By Captain Heath:* Can you give the names of the men who are anxious to go back? There is only one man I know of here now, Hendrey; he wanted to go down in the cutter, if you remember. One is now in New South Wales.

13. It has been asserted that men and the Government property there have been unfairly used for Mr. Jardine's private purposes; do you know anything about that? No.

14. You never saw any of it? No; I never saw anything of it at all.

15. Were you, as carpenter there, ever employed mending any private boats?—I do not mean any very small job? Oh, no.

16. You were not? No.

17. *By Mr. Drew:* You have seen no misappropriation of Government stores there in any way whatever? No; I did not.

18. Was the Government property well looked after while you were there? They were looked after as well as they could while I was there. We were short of material to do anything with.

19. Was Brown, the coxswain, there when you were there? He only just came down a short time before I left.

20. Have you had any conversation with men from Cape York since your time there? No, sir.

21. You have read the various statements in the papers, I suppose, about the management of Cape York? Yes.

22. From your twelve months' experience there do you believe there is truth in those statements? No; I don't. You allude to those paragraphs of Cockerill's?

23. Yes? I do not place the slightest faith in a word of them; I said, at the time, I thought it was his usual propensities breaking out. It seems to be a family failing amongst them; both him and his sons.

24. *By the Chairman:* What do you mean by family failing? Creating mischief.

CAPTAIN DAVID DRING recalled and further examined.

Capt. David Dring.

31 Dec., 1873.

1. *By the Chairman:* I think, Captain Dring, the principal point you came about to-day is in respect to this copper.—I understand from the Secretary that you have some further information to give respecting it.—The Secretary applied to the Custom House, and all he could get was this—the entry inwards of the steamer "Wainui," of the 29th of April, 1872,—which gives no information of any use whatever? It is a very extraordinary thing; the Collector of Customs told me, if you sent down he would give all the information; and I stated to him the information that was required. I find that 32 tons 14 cwt. of copper was shipped in the "Storm King" on the 1st of August, 1872.

2. Do you know what vessel brought it here? You have it here in this entry of the "Wainui."

3. It says, "Quantity unknown."—Is that the same? You can see by the date, I dare say. It was transhipped in August.

4. Are you aware from what vessel it was transhipped? No.

5. Is there anything further? It was shipped by Berens Banneger, I believe; but it is written in such a way that I made out the name to be "Bernard Lenneger." There was another four tons went down to Sydney, to Captain Towns, direct, and I am informed Mr. Jardine drew against that.

6. Have you any further statement to make? I wish to state that my boats at Somerset have been used several times for the purpose of fishing, and my seine has been used also there; that Mr. Jardine's boat has been used also several times with my seine.

7. *By Captain Heath:* Who looked after these boats of yours at Somerset? Mr. Brown.

8. Were they kept in the Government boat-shed? That I don't know; I believe they were.

9. *By Mr. Drew:* By whom were the boats used fishing? By Mr. Brown.

10. The person in charge? Yes.

11. By fishing you mean drawing the seine on the beach? Yes, on the beach; therefore, I thought they might as well have let my boats go and get pearl-shell.

FRANK LASCELLES JARDINE examined.

F. L. Jardine, Esquire.

31 Dec., 1873.

1. *By the Chairman:* Mr. Jardine, the Board have now heard all the evidence we are likely to get, and I will now ask you to make any statement in reply that you may wish or think necessary? I shall commence with Captain Dring. Captain Dring sent two boats and stores up to Edmonds Brown, at that time coxswain of the water police at Somerset. These boats were intended to be employed pearl shelling, but as Brown was holding an appointment in the Government service, he could not apply to me for a license, and did not do so. The stores were sold by Brown, and the proceeds were, I believe, transmitted to Captain Dring. The boats are still there.

2 Do you know to whom the stores were sold? A quantity were sold to the "Springbok."

3. To different people, I suppose? Yes; to different people about; I did not bother myself about the matter. Now, with regard to Cockerill. I think the charges made in the papers by J. T. Cockerill have been sufficiently contradicted by the evidence of witnesses, given on oath, during the inquiry held before the police magistrate, at Somerset, and the officers of H.M.S. "Beagle." Cockerill, in his evidence, states

F. L. Jardine, Esquire. 31 Dec., 1873.

states that Brown has boats employed pearl shelling; also, that a Government boat, condemned by Captain Moresby, has been repaired, and has been used for private purposes. Both of these statements are incorrect, as Brown has no boats, and since the condemnation of the police boat she has never been afloat. He also states that Brown was receiving four salaries. This, also, is incorrect, as Brown receives merely coxswain's pay, and £12 a-year for acting as postmaster, and nothing for acting as storekeeper, although Cockerill said he is paid £20. It has been shown by the evidence of McArthur that there were neither boats nor natives on the beach at Somerset during the 23rd or 24th of December; therefore, the statement made by Cockerill, must be untrue. With regard to the copper. In the early part of 1872, the s.s. "Wainui" visited Torres' Straits, expressly to procure copper jettisoned from the ship "Orford"; and the thirty tons of copper alluded to is the copper that was got by her, which, of course, I had no share in.

4. *By Mr. Drew:* No interest whatever? None; rather the reverse. When she was passing Somerset I would have seized the copper if I could have caught the "Wainui." I had a boat out after her, but there was a strong tide and we could not catch her. I would have seized it in my capacity as receiver of wreck. Referring to the seizure of a boat belonging to Delargy, Dare, and Tait, I may state that the boat came in unlicensed, after being cautioned, and was seized and sold under "*The Customs Act.*" The seizors took an inventory of everything on board the boat, which inventory was copied into the police journal on the station; and all the things were sold. Cockerill says no inventory was taken. The statement by Cockerill that he saw her tanned sails on board the "Vampire" is false; the "Vampire" never had tanned sails. No stores have been condemned at Somerset since the visit of His Excellency and the Colonial Secretary to Somerset, when they condemned stores that required condemning. The quarterly store returns can be referred to for information on that point. I distinctly deny Cockerill's statement, that he saw meat going down to the boats on the 24th of December. I deny that he ever saw any meat go down to the boats.

5. *By the Chairman:* I read in the letter addressed to you by Mr. Palmer, dated the 22nd of August, 1873, the following paragraph:—

"I regret to say that, from information of a semi-official nature which has reached this Government, there is too much reason to believe that, for some time past, you have been engaged in the pearl-shell fishery on your own account without the consent or privity of the Government."—Have you anything to state with regard to that? I have answered that in my letter.

6. Do you refer to this letter, dated the 29th of November, 1873, addressed to the Colonial Secretary? Yes.

7. Do I understand you to declare before the Board that that is a true and correct statement of the matter? Yes. I put this letter in as evidence. [*Vide Separate Appendix A, Enclosure No.* 8.]

8. *By Captain Heath:* Mr. Cockerill states that the Governor and Mr. Palmer were your two sureties for the license—Is that the case? No; it is untrue.

The Board adjourned *sine die.*

APPENDICES.

SEPARATE APPENDIX A.

Colonial Secretary's Office,
Brisbane, 8th December, 1873.

Sir,

I am directed to inform you that you have been appointed, in conjunction with the Under Secretary to the Treasury, and the Portmaster, to examine and report upon all matters and things connected with certain statements that have been circulated in the public papers respecting the management of the Harbor of Refuge, at Somerset, and the part alleged to have been taken by Mr. Frank Jardine, Police Magistrate, at Somerset, in the pearl-shell fisheries referred to in the correspondence of Captain Moresby, of H.M.S. "Basilisk"; and I am to request that you will be good enough to place yourself in communication with Mr. Drew and Captain Heath, with the view of taking necessary action at your earliest convenience.

The papers and correspondence in connection with the Inquiry, enumerated in the accompanying Schedule, are transmitted herewith.

I have, &c.,
H. H. MASSIE.

The Honorable H. G. Simpson, Brisbane.

SUSPENSION OF MR. F. JARDINE FROM OFFICE AS POLICE MAGISTRATE, SOMERSET.
(*Papers and Correspondence respecting*)

I.—Letter from the Colonial Secretary to His Excellency the Governor. 29th August, 1873.

Enclosure in No. I.

1. Copy letter from the Colonial Secretary to Mr. Jardine. 22nd August, 1873.

Sub-enclosures.

1. Copy of *Telegraph* newspaper. 28th July, 1873.
2. Copy of *Brisbane Courier*. 7th August, 1873.
3. Copy of *Telegraph* newspaper. 9th August, 1873.

II.—Copy of letter from Commodore Stirling to His Excellency The Marquis of Normanby. 10th September, 1873.

Enclosure in No. II.

1. Extract from letter from Captain Moresby, H.M.S. "Basilisk," to Commodore Stirling. 15th March, 1873.

III.—Copy of Executive Minute. D—4-10-73.
*IV.—Copy of Executive Minute. B—14-10-73.

Enclosure

* Not Printed.

Enclosures in No. IV.

1. Letter from the Police Magistrate, Somerset, to the Portmaster, Brisbane, 14th June, 1873, with memo. thereon by Captain Heath. 10–9–73.
2. Letter from T. G. Chapman to the Portmaster, complaining of the master of the "Lizzie Jardine." 9th September, 1873.

V.—Letter from the Under Colonial Secretary to Mr. Jardine. 16th October, 1873.

VI.—Letter from the Under Colonial Secretary to Mr. Charles Edward Beddome. 15th October, 1873.

VII.—Telegram from Mr. F. Jardine to the Colonial Secretary. 14th September, 1873.

VIII.—Letter from Mr. F. Jardine to the Colonial Secretary, in explanation of charges. 29th November, 1873.

Appendices.

A1. Copy of letter from Police Magistrate, Somerset, to the Colonial Secretary. 27th August, 1872.

B2. Copy of letter in reply from Under-Colonial Secretary. 19th December, 1872.

IX.—Letter from Mr. F. Jardine to the Colonial Secretary.

Correspondence *re* seizure by Water Police of two boats found in possession of natives of Cocoanut Island, and sold.

I.

Colonial Secretary's Office,
Brisbane, 29th August, 1873.

MY LORD,

Certain injurious reports having recently been circulated respecting the management of the Harbor of Refuge, at Somerset, I have the honor to transmit, for Your Lordship's information, copy of a letter which I deemed it my duty to address to Mr. Jardine, the Police Magistrate in charge of the Establishment, on the subject.

I have, &c.,
A. H. PALMER.

His Excellency The Most Honorable The Marquis of Normanby.
&c., &c., &c.

[ENCLOSURE 1 IN No. I.]

Colonial Secretary's Office,
Brisbane, 22nd August, 1873.

SIR,

I desire to bring under your notice a statement relative to the management of the Establishment at Somerset, and a leading article on the same subject, that appeared in the *Telegraph* newspaper of 28th July last,—a copy of which is enclosed herewith. Your attention is also directed to a subsequent letter, published in the same paper, of the 9th August instant, signed "J. T. Cockerill," in reference to an article on the same subject that appeared in the *Brisbane Courier* of the 7th August instant, copies of which are also enclosed.

Although many of the statements made in the *Telegraph* may be unfounded, and others greatly exaggerated, I regret to say that, from information of a semi-official nature which has reached this Government, there is too much reason to believe that for some time past you have been engaged in the pearl-shell fishery on your own account, without the consent or privity of the Government; and it is quite evident that such a trade, even admitting it to be legally and properly conducted on your part, is wholly incompatible with your duties as a public officer, placed in a very peculiar position, and cannot, now that it has come to the knowledge of the Government, be for one moment allowed.

It is unnecessary to remind you that the principal part of your duties is to exercise a general supervision of British interests in Torres' Straits and the adjoining waters; and the cutter placed at your disposal was despatched in consequence of the representations made as to the increasing importance of the traffic on the coast of New Guinea and amongst the adjacent islands, caused by the discovery of pearl-shell; and it was supposed that the presence of this vessel would be, on the one hand, a check upon those engaged in the fisheries, and would put a stop to malpractices that were reported to exist, and, on the other, would afford protection to traders in those seas legitimately employed.

The duty of supervision cannot be conducted by you in a proper manner if you are personally engaged in the trade, and the traffic must, at once, be discontinued.

Pending the receipt of any communication, which I have reason to believe will be addressed by the Commodore of the Australian Station to His Excellency the Governor on the subject, I am not prepared to take any decisive action in the matter; but in the event of the statements to which your attention has been directed remaining uncontradicted, or being confirmed by the Commodore's despatch, I shall feel it my duty to recommend that you be suspended from your office, and called upon to show cause why you should not be dismissed from the Public Service.

I have, &c.,
A. H. PALMER.

The Police Magistrate, Somerset.

[SUB-ENCLOSURE 1 IN No. 1.]

"*Telegraph*," *28th July*, 1873.

HOW THE PORT OF SOMERSET (CAPE YORK) IS MANAGED.

A gentleman who recently visited the Settlement at Cape York has furnished us with the following statement as to "the manner in which the police are employed at the free port and harbor of refuge." As public journalists having a duty to fulfil to the country, and with a view that the Government may be induced to institute a searching inquiry into the alleged facts, we publish the statement:—

"There are at present five boats belonging to Mr. F. L. Jardine (and Co.), Police Magistrate of Somerset, Cape York, employed in the pearl fishery of Torres' Straits, Mr. Jardine being, as he says, the only person allowed to hold a license from the Queensland Government for that purpose.

"On the 24th of December, the following boats left Somerset for the Ormond Reefs, manned as follows:—

"Boat No. 1, the 'Vampire.'—E. L. Brown, coxswain and sergeant of the water police, is in charge of this boat. She is about 12 tons burthen, the property of F. L. Jardine and Co., and acts as tender to the fishing boats engaged in collecting pearl-shell, &c., on the reefs. She carries all provisions, trade, &c., to and from the reefs to the divers, and brings all pearl-shell, tortoise-shell, &c., &c., to Somerset. The pay the crew of this boat receives from the Queensland Government is as follows:—

"E. L. Brown's

	£
"E. L. Brown's pay as water policeman	104
Ditto, pay as postmaster	20
Ditto, pay as Government storekeeper	20
Ditto, pay as sergeant and coxswain	20
Blunt, as water policeman	104
Tinkle ditto	104
	£372

In addition to which they receive clothes, rations, medicines, *medical comforts*, and passage money to and from Cape York. The trip occupies from three weeks to a month. One of the men said—'I would not swear I have done one week's work for the Government for the last twelve months.'

"Boat No. 2, the 'Roepuneum.'—Mr. Charles Jardine is in charge of this boat. He says he is employed by the Queensland Government as stock-keeper and tender of the cattle belonging to them, for which he receives the pay of £80 per annum, rations, &c. He (Mr. Charles Jardine) further stated that he 'knew nothing more about the cattle than seeing them come in to be milked when he was at the Settlement, as he was nearly all the time away in the pearl fishing boats. When he was at the Settlement he had to clean trade, tobacco and tomahawks (Sundays included), ready to go into the boats. He hates pearl fishing, and would gladly leave it, to-morrow, if he had the chance. He does not receive one shilling extra for pearl fishing; all he gets is his pay from the Queensland Government as stock-keeper.' The crew consists of South Sea Islanders and natives of Cape York.

"Boat No. 3, the 'Restless.'—The coxswain of this boat is Johnny Murry, a half-caste (*the best diver in Torres' Straits*). Murry says he is sergeant of the native police, but 'Tiney' wears his stripes, and they call him sergeant. He is paid £42 per annum, and extras as sergeant, by the Queensland Government, but he has not done one day's work for the Government since March twelve months. He does not receive anything extra for pearl fishing. He often finds a patch of shell and leaves it, as he is not properly paid. If ever he gets clear of the Government he knows where to go and pick it up, and he would gladly leave if he were allowed to do so, but is not. The crew is the same as No. 2 boat.

"Boat No. 4, a blue boat.—The coxswain is a white man, waiting to be employed as water policeman, in place of one of the Tinkles, two shipwrecked sailors belonging to the 'Crown,' brig. He says he does not receive pay until he joins the police, but gets his rations.

"Boat No. 5, now laid up for painting.—The remainder of the white police (three) are constantly and nearly solely employed in making sails, fixing rigging, painting, and getting ready for the arrival of the pearl boats.

"When a boat arrives, the whole of the police, both black and white, are employed in hauling her up, stripping all the gear, &c. The native police cut firewood, bring water, provisions, trade, the Government drays and horses being used for this purpose. They take all pearl-shell, tortoise-shell, copper, &c., to Mr. Jardine's house, and convey the same to the beach when shipped for Sydney. A very small quantity is now and then sent to Brisbane, to the Queensland Government, but nine-tenths go to Sydney. On the 6th February, 4 tons 5 cwt. of copper, together with a lot of shell, went to Sydney by the 'Gleaner,' schooner, Captain Bowman.

	£
"Pay of white police (six)	684
Pay of nine native troopers (about) ...	400
	£1,084

"Besides clothes, rations, medicines, passage money, medical comforts, &c."

"LIST of Prices charged at the Government Stores, at the free Port and Harbor of Refuge, Somerset, Cape York :—

	£	s.	d.
Flour, per ton ...	28	0	0
Ration sugar, ditto	56	0	0
Tea, per lb.	0	5	0
Coffee, ditto	0	2	0
Mustard, ditto	0	2	0
Tobacco, ditto	0	5	0
Bacon, ditto	0	1	9
Cheese (colonial) ditto	0	1	9
Bottled fruits, per bottle	0	1	6
Jams, per tin	0	1	0
Sardines, ditto	0	1	0
Potatoes, per lb.	0	0	3
Rice, ditto	0	0	6

"The flour is quite unfit for food, the tea is very inferior, and the sugar is the common Queensland ration. There is no duty or freight to pay, as it is supposed to be a free port, and H.M.S. ships carry up the stores free of charge."

"*Telegraph*," *28th July*, 1873.

There is a strong popular disbelief in the value of Civil Service inquiries, and we must confess to sharing in the prejudice. Occasionally, the Board arrive at a decision adverse to the person whose conduct may be the subject of inquisition, but in such instances, the victim is generally some unfortunate underling who has no "friends at court," and who is regarded as a species of pariah whose presence in the service is objectionable. Whether farcical or not, however, it is highly necessary that such inquiries should be instituted; although the public generally gauge their value by the manner in which the Board is constituted, and often, and justly, arrive at the conclusion that the verdict was not exactly in accordance with the evidence. It would be well, we submit, if there was an occasional departure from what has become the stereotyped fashion of conducting inquiries in this colony, so that the investigation might be more rigid, and the results more satisfactory—not to the accused, but to those who are really his paymasters. If ever strict inquiry, by commission or otherwise, were needed, it is in the matter of the Cape York Settlement.

We publish in another column a statement made to us in writing by one who speaks with the most positive assurance of its truthfulness; and, from what we can learn, the Government have not been unaware of the manner in which the "free port and harbor of refuge" is being controlled by Mr. F. L. Jardine. That the "lines have fallen in pleasant places" for the Jardine family, there can be little doubt; and if they have turned the State into a "goodly heritage" perhaps there are some who, looking at the question from the mere standpoint of personal advantage, and not as a matter affecting public principle, would be inclined to commend them. But not so the community. First of all we have Mr. Jardine, sen., enjoying a very easy billet at Rockhampton; then Mr. F. L. Jardine,

Jardine, as Police Magistrate, and four or five other offices, at Cape York, where, if report be true, he carries on a pearl fishery; and there are two others of the family quartered on the public, one of whom is stationed at Cape York. Altogether, a neat little sum is drawn by the family every year from the public Treasury, and nobody would find fault with the fact if it were believed that the money was earned; or, if there were any special claims entitling them to peculiar petting and consideration at the hands of the Government, people might be disposed to wink at it. True, Messrs. F. and A. Jardine penetrated overland from Rockhampton to the Cape, but they sold their cattle and horses to the Government at excellent prices, especially the latter, and the colony gained no particular benefit. Visitors at Somerset state that Mr. F. Jardine occupies an almost autocratic position there; that he boasts of being safe from political attack while the present Government are in power; that he can, in fact, do just as he likes, with Mr. Palmer at his back.

That the Government are bound to uphold their officers until actually found to be in the wrong, we freely grant; but, if it were sought to mete out equal justice to all, why not pursue a different mode of inquiry to that now usually observed? If the statements which appear in our columns to-day be true, and evidence respecting them can be obtained in Brisbane at the present time, why not have the facts elicited? Let a Board be appointed composed of men of integrity and impartiality—*outside* the service—men whom the public would be bound to rely upon as just judges, unswayed either by personal friendship or that feeling of *esprit de corps* which is thought sometimes to bias our Civil Service investigations. If the statements be unfounded, it is only just to Mr. Jardine that he should have an opportunity of vindicating himself; if they can be sustained by evidence, his retention in the service would reflect discredit upon the Government, and cause masters of vessels to give our "free port" a wide berth.

[SUB-ENCLOSURE 2 IN No. 1.]

"*Brisbane Courier*," 7 *August*, 1873.

HOW THE PORT OF SOMERSET (CAPE YORK) IS MANAGED.

A statement under the above heading, from a gentleman who recently visited the Settlement at Cape York, appeared in the columns of our evening contemporary of the 28th ultimo. The statement was to the effect that Mr. F. L. Jardine (Police Magistrate) and "Co." had five boats employed in pearl fishing; that Mr. Jardine was the only person allowed to hold a license from the Queensland Government for that purpose; that the white police were employed in this trade instead of performing their proper duties at the Settlement; and that Mr. Jardine charges extravagant prices for such provisions as he furnishes to shipwrecked or distressed mariners who call there for supplies. The charges made are very serious ones, and in order to ascertain what amount of truth they contained, and how far the Government were cognizant of Mr. Jardine's proceedings, we applied to the Colonial Secretary yesterday for information on the subject. Such information as he possesses, he very readily placed at our disposal, and it amounts to this:—Within the last two months or so, the Colonial Secretary became aware, for the first time, that Mr. Jardine was collecting pearl-shell for trading purposes on his own account. There is no "Co." so far as can be ascertained at present. The information respecting Mr. Jardine's proceedings was not obtained officially, but immediate steps were taken to procure an official statement on the subject, in order to put a stop to the proceeding at once. For, although, so far as is yet known, Mr. Jardine is carrying on the business in a perfectly legal and legitimate manner, it is without leave from the Minister at the head of his department, and altogether at variance with the functions and duties of a police magistrate of the territory. Some years ago, while Lieutenant Chester was at Cape York, Mr. Jardine was directed by the Colonial Secretary to encourage, as far as practicable, friendly relations with the natives of New Guinea nearest to the Straits, and for that purpose certain articles of "trade" were supplied from the Colonial Stores, and forwarded to Mr. Jardine. On the arrival of these stores at Cape York, Mr. Jardine arranged with Mr. Chester to take charge of the "trade" and convey it to New Guinea, in accordance with the wishes of the Colonial Secretary. This was done, the result being that the "trade" was bartered for pearl-shell, which realised about four times the Brisbane Market value of the stores. The shell was sent down to Brisbane, sold, and one-half the proceeds were given to Mr. Chester, the other half being paid into the Consolidated Revenue Fund. This is the only case in which Mr. Jardine has had leave from the Colonial Secretary to trade in pearl-shell or anything else.

With respect to the allegation that the police at Somerset are taken from their proper duties to be employed in pearl-shell fishing, the Colonial Secretary has no information, but is decidedly of opinion that it has no foundation in fact. The Sergeant of the Water Police, and others said to be so engaged, have made no complaint whatever, nor intimated to the Commissioner or any other officer of the department to which they belong, that they are, or ever have been, so engaged, although they have had opportunities of making such complaints if they had desired to do so. When His Excellency the Governor visited Cape York in the "Kate," steamer, last year, the Colonial Secretary who accompanied him asked the men if they had any complaint to make, and they all said they had not. They made no complaint at that time, and have made none since. The Mr. Charles Jardine said to be in charge of the second boat, is not in the pay of the Government, either as stockkeeper or in any other capacity; and all the expenditure on the Cape York Settlement appears on the Estimates which are voted by Parliament every Session.

The only remaining charge which it seems necessary to notice here, is that respecting the prices demanded for stores supplied to shipwrecked or distressed mariners. It is obvious that in a case like this, where a Government officer is in charge of an isolated settlement, a thousand miles from the head of his department, and where communication can only be secured at rare and uncertain intervals, very much must be left to the judgment and discretion of the officer, as to how he acts in particular cases. The general instruction Mr. Jardine has received, however, is to make no charge whatever for any provisions supplied to shipwrecked or distressed seamen calling at the Settlement; and, in the case of passing vessels short of provisions, to barter, and not to sell them on cheque or order. The wisdom of this course was demonstrated to us in a very striking manner yesterday at the Colonial Secretary's office, in the shape of a formidable bundle of dishonored cheques and orders for payment for provisions so supplied. Among the number was the cheque, for three pounds odd, of the gentleman who furnished our contemporary with the statement under notice. It seems that owners of vessels, as a rule, with very few exceptions, refuse to honor the cheques given to the Police Magistrate at Somerset for provisions supplied to their ships, no matter under what circumstances they may have been given.

It is satisfactory to learn that the charges made against Mr. Jardine, are not likely to prove anything like so serious as they at first sight appeared, and that prompt action has been taken to have the matter thoroughly inquired into with a view to remove all reasonable ground of complaint, and correct any irregularities which have been committed. We maintain the Settlement at Cape York for the benefit of our neighbors, to an enormous extent more than for any advantage we derive, or are ever likely to derive from it, and it would be an intolerable blunder and a disgrace to allow it, by mismanagement, to lose its character and usefulness, much less to become a private trading station carried on at the public expense.

"*The*

"The Telegraph," Saturday, 9th August, 1873.

Recapitulating the lame defence of Mr. F. Jardine, which we copied from our contemporary in our Thursday's issue, it may be summed up thus:—The Colonial Secretary has become aware, within the last two months, that Mr. Jardine was carrying on the pearl-fishing business, and has taken steps to put a stop to such proceedings. The Government have "no information" that the "police at Somerset are taken from their proper duties to be employed in pearl-shell fishing," but the Colonial Secretary is "decidedly of opinion that it (the statement) has no foundation in fact," apparently basing the opinion on the circumstance that the officers said to be so engaged have made "no complaint." It is averred that the Mr. Charles Jardine referred to is *not* in the pay of the Government; and as to the prices charged for stores, it appears that the tariff is left solely to the "judgment and discretion of the officer in charge."

It is simply upon public grounds that we return to this subject, believing as we do that the Government have—perhaps unwittingly—been aiding in the establishment of a private pearl-fishing business, chiefly at the public cost, by the manner in which Mr. Jardine has been virtually shielded from time to time, when any attempt has been made to furnish the information which the Colonial Secretary has been so tardy in receiving. In another column we publish a further statement in reply to the semi-official defence, and to this the writer attaches his name; and we can vouch, from personal knowledge, that there are other masters of vessels in port who can corroborate most of the allegations contained in the first article we published, and are assured that the pearl-fishing business carried on was well known along the coast, and in the neighboring colonies.

What the "steps" may be which Mr. Palmer is going to take to put an end to the proceedings, can only be conjectured, but the public will not be satisfied unless the inquiry is something more than a mere pretence, seeing how rooted has become the idea that Mr. Jardine is such an "official pet," that he can do as he likes. Just to show how much this feeling has been fostered, it may be mentioned that when Mr. Jardine was first in Government employ, and had been only twelve months in office, he obtained from the Lilley Government leave of absence for three months on half-pay. Just about the time that term expired Mr. Palmer became Mr. Lilley's successor. The latter had properly refused to give more than half-pay for the three months, or to extend the leave. Can the Colonial Secretary inform us how it was that the three months were extended to twelve, and *full pay* allowed for the whole time, even the three months remaining half which Mr. Lilley had refused. We have been assured that this statement is true, by persons who have perused documentary evidence in the shape of official figures. Again, after Mr. Jardine had twice missed his passage to Somerset by the usual method of communication, was not a small schooner chartered to take him up, together with twelve tons of flour, at a cost of £470? and did not those who were to have returned in her object to sail, owing to the absence of proper accommodation on board? The amount mentioned was paid, for we have it from the captain himself. These are not the only instances which might be adduced of the manner in which the Police Magistrate at Somerset has been petted and favored by his official superiors.

Mr. Palmer must surely be attempting the serio-comic business when he avers that he does not credit the report about the misemployment of the police because "no complaint" has been made. There are men in Brisbane now who laugh at the idea of complaining when all their efforts to do so have been thwarted; and one states that he would not have stayed in Somerset for £1,000 after the "Kate" left, if he had then told all he knew. Outside the swathing bands of red tape, no one would arrive at the conclusion that men were satisfied because they did not complain, when a murmur on their part might be serious in its consequence to them.

The wording of the last paragraph of the semi-official defence justifies the inference that a foregone conclusion has already been arrived at. It reads:—"It is satisfactory to learn, that the charges made against Mr. Jardine are not likely to prove anything like so serious as they at first sight appeared, and that prompt action has been taken to have the matter thoroughly inquired into," &c. If no inquiry has been made, how can it be so authoritatively affirmed that the charges are "not likely to prove anything like *so serious;*" but we can well understand that they are not likely to prove so if Mr. Palmer is going to institute inquiry after the usual fashion. If he is merely going to send the statement we published to Mr. Jardine for his "report," and accept that document as gospel truth when he receives it, the charges will assuredly *not* prove "so serious." The result might be somewhat different if evidence were sought where it may readily be found, and testimony, moreover, that the parties are willing to give *on oath*, if required.

[SUB-ENCLOSURE 3 IN No. I.]

"Telegraph," 9th August, 1873.

THE CAPE YORK SETTLEMENT.

TO THE EDITOR OF THE "TELEGRAPH."

SIR,

Within the last two months or so the Colonial Secretary became aware, for the "first time," that Mr. F. Jardine was collecting pearl-shell for trading purposes on his own account, and he states that there is no "Co.," so far as can be ascertained at present.

It appears very strange that the Colonial Secretary was not aware of this fact before, as it has been well known to all the masters of vessels in Torres' Straits for two years. At the time His Excellency and the Colonial Secretary visited Cape York, or rather Somerset (Cape York is eight miles west), the pearl-shell business was in full working order, and two or three of the water police, now in Brisbane, were employed in the boats for that purpose. There are also three masters of vessels now in port that testify to the same; that they have been in company with the boats mentioned in my first communication, both at Murry, Darnley, and the Warrior. In the two former places they procured cocoanuts, yams, bananas, &c., for food for the crews of the various boats. I saw Brown in charge of the "Vampire," and another boat on Cocoanut Island, in February last, seeking provisions there.

If the Colonial Secretary is "not aware," and actually disbelieves that Mr. Jardine is carrying on the pearl fishing business, how can he say there is no "Co."? The general opinion is that he knows more about this matter than he wishes others to know, and it does appear strange that he has just found it out, when it has been known in all these colonies for nearly two years. Does he know anything about 4 tons 5 cwt. of ingots of copper that went to Sydney by the "Gleaner," Captain Bowman, on the sixth of February last? Where it was got? What boats brought it to Somerset? And what crew were in the boats, or where it was kept afterwards?

With respect to the allegations that the police of Somerset are taken from their proper duties to be employed in pearl-shell fishing, the Colonial Secretary has "no information. but is decidedly of opinion that it has no foundation in fact." How is it that the Colonial Secretary did not find this fact out before? Surely he could have done so from the person who informed him that Mr. Jardine was carrying on the business on his own private account. Had he wished to do so, positive information could have been obtained at once, if necessary, but he simply says, "I don't believe it." There are, at present, two of the water police of Somerset in Brisbane who have been twelve months under Mr. Jardine. They state they have been employed the whole of their time in pearl fishing. I am informed that most of the discharged police of Somerset have, from time to time, endeavored to bring this matter before the Government, but have always met with rejoinders in this style:—"What business is it of yours how you were employed at Somerset, so long as you receive your pay? Did you expect you were to do nothing? The Police Magistrate has his instructions, and acts accordingly, and the less you say in this matter the better it will be for yourself. We want to hear no complaints from Somerset. Mr. Jardine is a good and efficient officer, and does his duty to the satisfaction of the Government."

The

The sergeant of the water police and others said to be so engaged have "made no complaint whatever." Just fancy these poor men, under the stern rule of Mr. F. L. Jardine, making complaints to the Colonial Secretary of being employed for weeks at a time in pearl fishing, and then expect to live in Somerset afterwards. The idea is monstrous. One of them said this morning he would not have been left at Somerset after that for £1,000, as he would not have considered himself safe one day after the "Kate" had left—as the Colonial Secretary observes, "one thousand miles from Brisbane, with very doubtful communication." But let Sergeant T. E. Brown once land in Brisbane, and he will then tell you how many months he has been employed in the "Vampire" and other pearl fishing boats. He will be able to tell you how the condemned stores, boats, &c., are disposed of. In fact, he can, and I believe will, what is generally termed "let the cat out of the bag."

On the shipwrecked mariners' topic nothing was ever said by me; but this I know—they are compelled to work, fencing, &c., or they only get sufficient rations to keep them alive.

As to the list of prices charged for provisions, that published by me was from an account rendered at the Government Stores at Somerset, a copy of which is hung up in the store for inspection. That Mr. Jardine has a "discretionary power" I have no doubt, as I heard him tell Routledge if he made any complaints he would charge 1s. per pound for flour next time.

It is stated that Mr. C. Jardine is not on the Government books. This is very likely, but there is no doubt he receives his pay from the Queensland Government, and Mr. C. Jardine has told others, *besides myself*, that he is paid £80 per annum, and receives no other pay; he believes that he receives the £80 for being stockman.

I totally deny the assertion of the Colonial Secretary, saying he has in his possession a dishonored cheque belonging to the writer of the former article. If he has, there is no necessity to publish it in the newspapers, as he has his remedy.

Lastly.—Is the Colonial Secretary aware that the natives of Cape York, both women and men, are taken to Murry and Darnley, both South Sea Islanders, and of course outside the boundary of the colony, contrary to the Act of Parliament, and that part of the crew are natives of these islands, and are brought within the colony contrary to the law? There are three boats that have one woman each—Johnny Murry's boat and two others, all being natives of Cape York.

The pilot boat lately built by the Government of Queensland, and called the "Lizzy Jardine," is exactly what is required by Mr. F. Jardine; and as there is no use whatever for a pilot at Cape York, she will answer for other purposes admirably well. The houses at Somerset can be plainly seen seven or eight miles out at sea, and as the Albany Pass is both wide and deep, there is no use for a pilot cutter to or from Somerset.

Yours, &c.,
J. T. COCKERILL.

II.

"Clio," at Sydney,
10th September, 1873.

MY LORD MARQUIS,

With reference to my letter dated 23rd August, 1873, I have the honor to forward for your Lordship's information, a copy of a report from Captain Moresby, of H.M.S. "Basilisk," concerning the Pearl-shell Fisheries in Torres' Straits; wherein reference is made to Mr. Jardine (Police Magistrate) being engaged in pearl-shell fishing.

I have, &c.,
T. H. STIRLING,
Commodore.

His Excellency The Most Honorable The Marquis of Normanby, &c., &c., &c.,
Governor of Queensland.

ENCLOSURE 1 IN No. II.

Relative to Pearl-shell and Bêche-de-Mer Fisheries.

"Basilisk," Somerset,
Cape York, 15th March, 1873.

SIR,

With reference to the fifth paragraph of my sailing orders, directing me to collect and report all the reliable information obtainable respecting the development of the pearl-shell and bêche-de-mer fisheries, and the treatment of the natives employed thereon.

I have the honor to make the following report.

The fishing stations are as follows :—

1. Somerset, Cape York, Pearl Shelling Station.

* * * * * * *

Decked Vessels at present in Torres' Straits employed on the Fisheries.

Name.	Owners.	Description.	Port.
"Vampire"	F. L. Jardine, P.M.	Decked boat, 8 tons	Somerset.
* * *	* * *	* * *	* * *
* * *	* * *	* * *	* * *

Polynesian Native Laborers now in Torres' Straits.

No.	Employers.	Port.
5	F. L. Jardine	Cape York.
*	* * * *	* * *

Particulars

Particulars respecting the present state of each Station.

1. *Somerset.*—Mr. F. L. Jardine, Police Magistrate, owner of three large open boats and the decked boat "Vampire;" has in his employ forty natives, of whom five are Polynesians, and thirty-five natives of Cape York or Torres' Straits Islands. These boats are provided with regular legal papers, signed by Mr. Jardine in his capacity as a magistrate and custom house officer; one of the boat's papers is signed by Mr. Palmer, Prime Minister of Queensland. These boats are constantly employed pearl shelling.

* * * * * * * *

At present the only boats employed are those of Mr. Jardine, the Police Magistrate at Somerset.

Colin Thompson and other white men on the islands have applied to Mr. Jardine for a license to fish in Queensland waters, but Mr. Jardine states he is unable to grant their request, as they cannot find bonds for security. This is to be regretted.

* * * * * * * *

I have further to report, that since writing the above, Mr. Jardine has informed me that he has granted the man Colin Thompson, of Cocoanut Island, a license to fish for pearl-shell. This is a step in the right direction.

I have, &c.,
J. MORESBY,
Captain.

Commodore J. H. Stirling, Senior Officer.

III.

COPY OF MINUTES OF PROCEEDINGS OF THE EXECUTIVE COUNCIL ON 4 OCTOBER, 1873. *Re* MR. JARDINE, POLICE MAGISTRATE, AT SOMERSET, &c.

D.
Approved:
NORMANBY.
4-10-73.

His Excellency the Governor, at the instance of the Honorable the Attorney-General for the Colonial Secretary, submits to the Council papers and correspondence relating to a trade in the Torres Straits' Pearl-shell Fisheries, reported to be carried on by Mr. Frank Jardine on his own account, without the consent or privity of the Government.

As it appears from an extract from Captain Moresby's letter, enclosed in Commodore Stirling's despatch of 10th September last, to His Excellency the Governor, that Mr. Jardine, at the time Somerset was visited by Captain Moresby, in H.M.S. "Basilisk," had one decked boat and five open boats employed in the trade, all provided with papers purporting to be regular legal papers, signed by Mr. Jardine, in his capacity as a magistrate and custom house officer, and manned by 35 natives of Cape York and Torres Straits' Islanders, and five Polynesians.

It also appears by a letter of 22nd August last, from the Colonial Secretary to Mr. Jardine, that Mr. Jardine, if engaged at the time alleged in the Pearl-shell Fishery, on his own account, was so engaged without the consent or privity of the Government.

The Council deliberate and advise in terms of the intimation conveyed to Mr. Jardine in the letter referred to, that he be suspended from all the duties and functions of his office as Police Magistrate and person in charge of the Harbor of Refuge, at Somerset, and that he be called upon to show cause why he should not be dismissed from the Public Service.

The Council further advise that some fit and competent person be appointed to act in Mr. Jardine's place temporarily, and to do all things that may be required of him as the officer in charge of the establishment, and that the person appointed, and the letter suspending Mr. Jardine, be forwarded by the first opportunity.

A. V. DRURY, Clerk of the Council.

The Honorable The Colonial Secretary, &c., &c., &c.

V.

M—73-368.

Colonial Secretary's Office,
Brisbane, 16th October, 1873.

SIR,

Adverting to a letter from this office of 22nd August last, relating to certain injurious reports at that time in circulation respecting the management of the Harbor of Refuge at Somerset under your charge, and to the trade in the Torres' Straits pearl-shell fisheries, in which you were said to be engaged on your own account and without the privity of the Government, I am directed to inform you, that the Government are now in possession of an official communication on the subject from Captain Moresby, of H.M.S. "Basilisk," to Commodore Stirling, which places it beyond a doubt that you have been extensively engaged in the trade, whilst there is reason to believe that you have taken advantage of your official position to give an exclusive privilege to the boats owned by yourself to fish for pearl-shell in excess of your powers, and without any authority whatever.

The action taken by yourself cannot fail to be prejudicial to you in your capacity as a public officer, more especially as regards the peculiar position you hold at Somerset. The Government, therefore, have thought it necessary to mark their disapproval of the course you have pursued in the strongest manner, and I am directed to inform you that you are now called upon to show cause why you should not be dismissed from the public service, and that, in the meantime, you are suspended from all the duties and functions of your office as Police Magistrate at Somerset, and all other offices held in conjunction therewith.

An officer will be immediately appointed to relieve you and take charge of the establishment, which will form the subject of a separate communication.

Duplicate copies of the former letter of the 22nd August last, with enclosure, are forwarded for your information, as also copy of the correspondence of Captain Moresby, to which allusion has been made.

I have, &c.,
H. H. MASSIE.
Under Colonial Secretary.

Frank L. Jardine, Esquire, Somerset, Cape York.

VI.

M-73-629.

Colonial Secretary's Office,
Brisbane, 15th October, 1873.

SIR,

Circumstances having occurred which have rendered it necessary that Mr. Frank Jardine, at present Police Magistrate and officer in charge of the Harbor of Refuge at Somerset, should be suspended from office, I am directed to inform you that His Excellency the Governor, with the advice of the Executive Council, has been pleased to appoint you Police Magistrate at Somerset, with full power to act in the place of Mr. Jardine, and to have the general charge of the Settlement during his suspension, or until such other arrangements are made as the Government may resolve upon.

Your salary during the time you hold the office will be at the rate of one guinea a-day, with travelling allowance at the same daily rate.

As

As it is necessary that Mr. Jardine should be relieved at once, application for your passage has been made to the officer in command of Her Majesty's ship "Beagle," now lying in this port, and which will sail for Somerset not later than Saturday next. You will therefore have your arrangements completed to proceed by her on that day.

Mr. Jardine has been informed as to the cause which has led to his being suspended, and he has been instructed to deliver over to you all buildings, boats, stores, arms, books, and office records, and Government property of every description.

You will make a complete inventory, in duplicate, of all property delivered to you by Mr. Jardine—one copy to be forwarded to this office, and the other to be retained by yourself.

You will report fully, for the information of the Government, upon all matters that come under your notice in respect of the Settlement, with such remarks and observations as you may deem requisite.

Circumstances having transpired which lead the Government to believe that Dugald McArthur, master of the Government schooner "Lizzie Jardine," is unfit to take charge of her, you will make a strict inquiry as to his competency, and other qualifications, for his present appointment, and particularly as regards the occasion of his getting his vessel aground upon a small island between "Halfway" and Somerset, reported by Mr. Jardine in June last.

In the event of your not being satisfied as to his fitness for his present situation, in every respect, you have full authority to dismiss him at once, and you will then take the schooner under your own charge, and make such arrangements as may be necessary until another master is appointed.

You will carefully carry out the instructions previously issued to your predecessors, with the provisions of which you are expected to make yourself acquainted.

A copy of a letter having reference to these instructions, from this office, to Mr. Jardine, under date 11th May, 1870, is enclosed for your information. Since that date a trade has sprung up in the pearl-shell fishery, which requires very careful supervision, and it will be your duty, so far as you have the power of control, to see that no irregularities are committed, and that no natives are detained, or employed, against their will, by persons engaged in the trade.

With regard to licenses, which appear to have been granted, or considered necessary to be issued by Mr. Jardine, to boats or vessels employed in the fishery, it is proper to point out that there is no Act in force regulating the pearl fisheries, or under which a license is required, or can be granted.

Persons engaged in the trade are responsible for their own actions, and must avoid the performance of any act contrary to law.

No boats or men employed by, or belonging to, the Government establishment, are to be allowed to be engaged directly or indirectly in the pearl-shell fishery, or in the collection of bêche-de-mer, or other products, or to have any share or interest in such trade, on any pretence whatever; and any licenses issued to such boats are to be cancelled. Copies of "*The Kidnapping Act of* 1872," and of "*The Polynesian Laborers Act of* 1868," will be furnished for your information and guidance.

There is one other matter to which it is necessary that your attention should be directed, which has repeatedly been brought under the notice of Mr. Jardine, but which appears to have been disregarded. The stores and supplies forwarded from time to time to Somerset, are intended exclusively for the use of the persons employed on the establishment in the public service, and for the relief of shipwrecked persons, and are not intended to be supplied to trading vessels, or ships passing by under ordinary circumstances; but in the event of its being absolutely necessary to dispose of provisions, or stores of any kind, for the use of such vessels, other articles which may be useful to the Settlement, or of which you may stand in need, whenever practicable, should be taken in exchange, and payment should never be made in cheques or orders, which, on almost all occasions, are dishonored on presentation.

I have, &c.,
H. H. MASSIE,
Under Colonial Secretary.

Charles Edward Beddome, Esquire, &c., &c.

VII.

Telegram from The Police Magistrate, Somerset, *to* The Colonial Secretary, Brisbane.

Normanton, 14th October, 1873.

Received letter seventy-three (73) four one eight (418) to-day relative to management of Establishment at Somerset and will reply by first opportunity the enclosed forwarded for your information Copy We have never been employed pearl shelling by Mr Jardine Ed. L. Brown Coxn. W. Brooks W. Police H. D. Mills W. Police John Norman W. Police Frederick Dryer W. Police.

FRANK L. JARDINE,
Police Magistrate, Somerset.

The Honorable The Colonial Secretary, Brisbane.

VIII.

The Police Magistrate, Somerset, *to* The Colonial Secretary, Brisbane.

Brisbane, 29th November, 1873.

Sir,

I do myself the honor to acknowledge the receipt of your letters 22nd August and 16th October last, D-73-418 and M-73-638, with enclosures and extracts from newspapers, in which you state that there is reason to believe that I have taken advantage of my official position to give an exclusive privilege to boats owned by myself to fish for pearl-shell, in excess of my powers and without any authority whatever, and beg to offer the following explanation:—

In the latter part of 1872 my brother engaged in the pearl fishery with three boats (there being no one else interested directly or indirectly in them), for each of which he holds a license granted by me in my capacity of Sub-Collector of Customs, under the provisions of "*The Customs Act*;" but I was unaware of the existence of any such form as a "fishing license" for pearl-shell, beche-de-mer, &c., being requisite, and have, therefore, never issued any other than an ordinary boat license "to trade." My brother engaged a Captain Atkins to look after and work the boats, they being manned with native crews, viz.:—Two South Sea Islanders in each, the remainder of the crew being aboriginals. I myself have never been away in any of the boats, nor have I ever personally engaged in the fishery; indeed, the only occasion on which I have seen a shell picked up was when with His Excellency the Governor and yourself at Prince of Wales' Island.

That I have not in any way sought to interfere unjustly with those engaged in the pearl fishery is, I submit, abundantly proved by the testimony of all the masters of vessels in Torres Straits, who have been fishing there for the last two years. [*Vide paper A.*]

With reference to Captain Moresby's letter, which is, in reality, the only part of the charge against me worthy of serious refutation, I may observe that had that officer taken the same trouble to be correct in his statements as he appears to have done in collecting his information, he would have found that my brother, Mr. C. Jardine, was the owner of the boats. At the time of the "Basilisk's" arrival at Somerset, I believe the boats were on on the coast of New Guinea, their licenses, of course being in them; it was, therefore, impossible that I could have shown the licenses to Captain Moresby. He might also have learned that I had no authority whatever to grant or withhold *licenses to fish* in Queensland waters, and that the "Vampire" mentioned by him was never employed "pearl shelling."

On the "Basilisk's" arrival in Torres Straits, Captain Moresby himself prohibited all boats fishing that had not boat licenses, and among the number were boats belonging to the vessels "Western Star," "Melanie," "Woodbine," "Challenge," and "Crishna" seized by the "Basilisk" under "*The Kidnapping Act.*"

Colin Thompson and "others" did apply to me for boat licenses under "*The Customs Act,*" and not for licenses to fish; but in all cases where proper sureties were not forthcoming I refused to grant them, and I submit that in the terms of the Act I could not do otherwise. I gave these men every chance, and even advised them to telegraph from Normanton for the necessary sureties, and said that if any Government official "wired" me that bonds had been entered into to his satisfaction, I would grant provisional licenses at once. Several took advantage of this, but in the case of those who did not choose to do so (although Normanton was within five days sail, with a leading wind each way), I refused to establish a precedent by granting provisional licenses.

So far from afterwards granting a license to Colin Thompson, as stated by Captain Moresby, the Water Police, by my orders, seized two of his boats, that were illegally trading, which boats I sold by auction after the expiration of the time mentioned in the Act.

With regard to the "Vampire" you will, doubtless, remember that prior to March, 1872, I had made repeated representations of the necessity of sending a suitable craft for the Settlement, and finding at length that a vessel of some kind was absolutely necessary, I ordered the "Vampire" (about ten tons burthen), from Sydney, at my own expense; she arrived early in 1872, and from that time has been constantly employed on Government service, with a police crew, and was generally known throughout Torres Straits as the police boat. Until your arrival at Somerset, I was unable to procure a boat license for the "Vampire," as I had a delicacy in issuing one to myself, you kindly helped me out of the difficulty by signing it [*vide License*], which is merely an ordinary boat trading license, issued in terms of the customs' regulations, and not what I presume to be an imaginary one, viz., a license to fish. The log book kept by the coxswain or constable in charge of the boat during the trip (the correctness of which has been attested on oath), will prove that the "Vampire" was never engaged pearl shelling. On the arrival of the Queensland Government cutter "Lizzie Jardine," I sold the "Vampire," having no further use for her.

While on the subject of Captain Moresby's letter, I may mention that by a few thoughtless words, he so undermined my authority in the Straits, that it has taken months to neutralise their effect. He gave out, as his opinion, that agreements with natives and masters of vessels, made before me, at Somerset, were neither legal nor binding [*vide Correspondence*], while in my capacity of Shipping Master I was authorised to witness the shipment of men on the articles of agreement.

Referring to the letters of J. T. Cockerill, in the *Telegraph* newspaper, I may observe that the gross untruth of the statement that my brother, Mr. C. Jardine, was employed by the Government as stock-keeper, at a salary of £80 a year, a statement easily disproved by reference to the accounts, should cast great doubt on the credibility of his other statements.

The charges contained in his correspondence with the *Telegraph*, appear to me to resolve themselves, briefly, into the following:—

1. That I, as Police Magistrate, at Somerset, was engaged, personally, in the Pearl-shell Fishery.

Answer 1.—This has already been sufficiently explained.

2. That I employed the Government boats and men in prosecuting the fishery and in working the boats.

Answer 2.—The sworn evidence of all the Police at Somerset, taken before Mr. C. E. Beddome and the Commander of H.M.S. "Beagle," [*vide Paper marked C* *], is, I think, sufficient to dispose of this charge.

The Police have frequently asked permission to go away in the boats for a trip, as a change from the monotony of their life, but I invariably refused to allow them to do so, lest it should be said that I was employing Government men on private work.

With regard to Johnny Murray, a Maori half-caste; this man was in my employment for about three years, until the desertion of some of the troopers necessitated my placing him on the strength of the Queensland Native Police Force; during all this time he had been employed at Government work, looking after and protecting the cattle, and assisting to patrol the district. For upwards of a year my brother was also employed in the same manner, and during this time neither of them received any remuneration from the Government.

When my brother engaged in the pearl fishery, I permitted Johnny to accompany him in the boats, he being a sailor; but whenever his services were required, he remained on shore. I ought, perhaps, to have removed him from the force when the necessity for his services no longer existed, but seeing that the Government had had the benefit of his services and those of my brother for so long, as well as the use of my boat, I could see no harm in permitting him to accompany my brother. He is no longer in the force, nor has he been for some time past, but is still assisting in looking after the cattle and doing "Native Police duty" when required.

3. That, with the aid of Government boats and men, I procured a quantity of copper, which was afterwards sent to Sydney.

Answer 3.—In August, 1871, the ship "Oxford" grounded in Flinders' Passage, and hove overboard about 60 tons of copper to lighten her; she got off eventually, and abandoned the copper, a quantity of which I recovered and showed to you during your visit to Somerset, and offered to give it up to the Government, which you refused.

On the arrival of the steamer "Wainui," Captain Gay having informed me that he had purchased the copper from the Insurance Companies, I handed it over to him, and hold his receipt for the same. Before leaving Torres Straits, Captain Gay made over to me all "right and title" to the remainder of the jettisoned copper [*vide Paper marked D.*], and I have since recovered a portion of it.

4. It is insinuated that I made an improper use of condemned stores.

Answer—Since the survey of stores held by you in September, 1872, there have been no stores condemned, as my accounts will show.

5. That the men (Water Police) had complaints to make against me, but were afraid to do so.

Answer.—The sworn evidence referred to in charge 2 sufficiently refutes this.

In conclusion, I regret that the very short time that elapsed between the arrival of Mr. Beddome and my departure from Somerset precluded the possibility of an inquiry being held on the spot, where full evidence on all the subjects referred to in your letters and enclosures could have been obtained. I trust, however, that the documentary evidence now furnished is sufficient to prove that the more serious charges brought against me are without foundation; but as I cannot feel satisfied until these aspersions have been authoritatively and publicly contradicted, I beg respectfully that a full inquiry may be held.

I have, &c.,
FRANK L. JARDINE.

The Honorable The Colonial Secretary, Brisbane.

A.

* *Vide* Mr. Beddome's report, page 32.

A.

Somerset, 9th October, 1873.

I have been in Torres Straits since February this year, engaged in pearl-shell fishing, and testify hereby that I only saw Mr. Jardine's boats occasionally, sailing about—I have never been interfered with by them, and have received from Mr. Jardine all the aid in respect to my fishing which I could reasonably expect.

EDWIN REDLICH,
Master of the Schooner "Franz."

Schooner "Susannah Booth,"
Torres Straits, 30th August, 1873.

In reference to reports current about the Straits and otherwise, I hereby beg to state that I have been in command of a "pearl fishing" station belonging to Jas. Merriman, Esq., Sydney, for the term of nearly two years, during which time I have shelled in all parts of the Straits and also during that time can perfectly testify to the truth, that I have not seen any boats belonging to Mr. Jardine *a-shelling*, nor has he interfered in any way whatever with the above fishing station.

W. R. WARE,
Master and Superintendent of the above Stations.

Somerset, 1st October, 1873.

I, master of a vessel pearl shelling in Torres Straits, do hereby certify that Mr. Jardine has never in any way interfered with my shelling, but on the contrary, I have always found him prompt and willing to forward my own and other "pearlers'" interests.

R. SCOTT,
Master Schooner "Three Brothers."

Somerset, 30th August, 1873.

I have been owner of a pearl shelling vessel in Torres Straits for two years, and I hereby certify that Mr. Jardine has in no way obstructed or interfered with my shelling business, and I never saw his boats at work.

JOHN BELL,
Owner Schooner "Mary Anne Christina."

B.

"Susannah Booth," 9th May, 1873.

Captain McCourt,
"Enchantress," cutter.

DEAR SIR,

I have taken the liberty of writing to you in reference to two natives whose names are "Marwo" and "Calos," being now on board your vessel and under an agreement with me for a term of nine months as yet, which has been taken to "Cape York" duty stamp, and acknowledged to be perfectly legal by Mr. Jardine; those natives were given liberty to go to Cocoanut Island in my absence to Sydney, until my return, in the meantime I have no dought have gone with you, you not knowing they were under an agreement with me.

Hoping this will not give you any offence, and trusting you will let the natives return to their original employment to save any more trouble in the matter.

W. R. WARE,
Master, Warrior Island Station.

Cutter "Enchantress," 10th May, 1873.

Captain Ware,
Schooner "Susannah Booth."

DEAR SIR,

In reafrance to the two natives you speak off as Bean under an agreement with you. I will make it my Busness to see the Captn. of the Man o war, and if he says that an agreement stands good you can have them. But he has allready told us difrent conserning an agreement; however, I will see him and explain to him how long the natives has bean at work for you and how long they have bean on Cocoanut Island and fead by me. Wishing you all sorts of success I remain your truly

JOHN McCOURT.

Master in charge the cutter "Enchantress."

D.

I hereby transfer to Mr. Frank L. Jardine all right and title to any copper found in Torres Straits, or on board any vessel from this date, the same copper branded "Wallaroo," and jettissoned from the ship "Oxford," in August, 1871.

W. GAY,
Master s.s. "Wainui."

Port Albany, Somerset, 17th October, 1872.

APPENDIX A 1.

67-72.

Somerset, 27th August, 1872.

SIR,

I do myself the honor to inform you that I have recovered, and now have in my possession, about four (4) tons of (cake and ingot) copper. It was thrown overboard from the ship "Oxford," in August, 1871, close to "Wednesday" Island, where she got ashore.

I am unable to state in which office it was insured, but believe it was in Melbourne. Every cake and ingot is stamped "Wallaroo." I await your instructions concerning it.

I have, &c.,
FRANK L. JARDINE, P.M.

The Honorable The Colonial Secretary, Brisbane.

APPENDIX

APPENDIX B 2.

D-72-629.

Colonial Secretary's Office,
Brisbane, 19th December, 1872.

SIR,

With reference to your letter of the 27th August last, in which instructions are applied for as to the disposal of four tons of cake and ingot copper, part of the cargo of the ship "Oxford," thrown overboard in August, 1871, on her getting aground near Wednesday Island, and subsequently recovered by you. I have the honor to inform you that the Colonial Treasurer, to whom the matter was referred, advises that the same should be sold for the benefit of whom it may concern, and if not already disposed of, it had better be sent to Brisbane by the first opportunity and sold by public auction.

I have, &c.,
H. H. MASSIE.

The Police Magistrate, Somerset.

IX.

Somerset, 2nd September, 1873.

SIR,

I do myself the honor to inform you, that the two boats seized by the Water Police last June, the particulars of which were reported in my letter 110-73 of June 20th, were yesterday sold by auction. They were purchased by Captain Ware, on behalf of James Merriman, of Sydney, for the sum of fifty-nine pounds (£59), an order for which amount I beg to enclose.

I have, &c.,
FRANK L. JARDINE, P.M.

The Honorable The Colonial Secretary, Brisbane.

(2.)

Somerset, 20th June, 1873.

SIR,

I do myself the honor to inform you, that in consequence of information received, to the effect that three boats left last December on Cocoanut Island by William Walton, master of the barque "Crishna," were cruising about the Straits, manned solely by natives of Cocoanut and adjacent islands, with firearms in their possession, I despatched Coxswain Brown in the "Vampire," with orders to cruise among the islands in the North-east Channel, for the purpose of ascertaining whether the report was true or not, and in the event of finding boats, arms, or ammunition in possession of the natives, to seize and bring them into Somerset.

The "Vampire" returned yesterday with two boats, and reports that they have been visiting most of the islands, including Awreed, Stephens, Darnley, and Murray, manned entirely by Torres' Straits natives, and that at Darnley they had caused a quarrel in which a woman had her brains knocked out.

On the "Vampire's" arrival at Cocoanut Island the two boats were lying at anchor, one of them having just come in from a cruise, the third was absent, with a native crew, and could not be found; both boats have the names "Enchantress" and "Colin Thomson," painted on their sterns, but from what I hear, I think it is very doubtful as to whom they really belong; as previous to the "Crishna's" sailing from Cocoanut Island last December, I believe the master (Walton) entered into some arrangement concerning his boats and men with a man called Thomson, who is the owner of a small cutter named the "Enchantress." Thomson at that time was living on Cocoanut Island, but has lately moved his station and property to the Brothers' Hills, leaving Walton's (?) boats on the island with the natives, who, apparently, have lost little time in making use of them.

Another report states that Walton gave the boats to the natives in payment for a season's service on board the "Crishna," collecting bêche-de-mer; but, since the late exposures and seizures, emanating from "*The Kidnapping and Polynesian Laborers Acts*," a system of assisting and playing into each others' hands has come into vogue, amongst the small fry, who not having the requisite accommodation in their wretched little vessels, and being unable to pay the wages asked by Polynesians, are forced to trade among the islands in the Straits, and pick up a man here and there, who after being on board a few days takes advantage of the first favorable opportunity and deserts; it is, therefore, very difficult indeed to find out who is the *bona fide* owner of a boat, or employer of natives.

Walton, while master of the schooner "Matilda," left boats, arms, and ammunition with the Cocoanut islanders in December, 1871, and by so doing caused a great deal of trouble, as the boats were made use of for visiting the weaker islands, and the arms for killing and ill-using the inhabitants. (Referred to in my letter 2-72 of 2nd January, 1872.) During one of their visits to Dugong Island, about 30 miles from here, on which there remained only a few old men, women, and children (the young men being absent at the time on a Turtling expedition), they shot every soul on the island at the time.

In conclusion, I have the honor to inform you, that, as I imagine, there will be no claim put in for the boats as required by Section C. * of 9 Vic. No. 15. It is my intention, with your approval, to sell them by auction after the expiration of one calendar month from the date of seizure; merely allowing such time to elapse between the expiration of the month and day of sale, as will be sufficient for the notice thereof to gain publicity.

Trusting I have acted in accordance with your wishes,

I have, &c.,
FRANK L. JARDINE, P.M.

To The Honorable The Colonial Secretary, Brisbane.

SEPARATE APPENDIX B.

M.—73-774.

Colonial Secretary's Office,
Brisbane, 12th December, 1873.

SIR,

In addition to the papers and correspondence in connection with the inquiry respecting the management of Somerset, forwarded on the 8th December instant, I have the honor to enclose the Report of Mr. Beddome on taking charge of the Establishment, also the official log kept by the coxswain of the Water Police boat from the 8th June, 1872, to the 25th June, 1873.

I have, &c.,
H. H. MASSIE.

The Honorable H. G. Simpson, Chairman.

Somerset,

Somerset, 11th November, 1873.

SIR,

I have the honor to report for your information that I arrived here in H.M.S. "Beagle" on the evening of the 5th instant, and received charge of the Settlement from Mr. Jardine on the 7th.

On my arrival, Mr. Jardine informed me that the natives, both on the mainland and islands, had been committing murder and depredations; a pearl-sheller's camp eight (8) miles from the Settlement was attacked, and a man named James Atkins brutally murdered.

All the native missionaries from New Guinea, Cornwallis, and Saibai, came into the Settlement, having been driven away by the natives. They left their wives and children on one of the islands, their boat not being large enough to bring them in safety to Somerset. Mr. Jardine, at the request of Mr. Murry (European Missionary here), let him have the cutter, he going in it, to try and settle the difference between the natives and missionaries. He has not returned yet.

Two parties were sent by sea and one by land to hunt up the murderers of James Atkins, who sent a message into the Settlement that they intended to attack it and kill everyone in the place. Some natives were seen that night both at the Police Magistrate's house and the barracks; they cut the throat of one of the horses and retired without doing any other damage.

Some of the pearl-shellers requested Mr. Jardine to allow them to join the parties that he sent out, which he did; they encountered the natives about thirty miles from here, who were in large force and showed a most determined resistance. I am thankful to report that they were properly dispersed; one of the native troopers received a spear in the side, which was, fortunately, turned by a rib, or it would have proved fatal, as it is he will be unfit for duty for some weeks; others of the party received spears through their clothes. It is to be hoped that the prompt action in this case will prevent any more depredations.

Mr. Jardine informs me that there are large numbers of the natives of the mainland and adjacent islands employed by the pearl-shellers as divers. These men have been brought before him by the shellers, and when he found that they were willing to be shipped, he has placed them on the ship's articles, the captains making a proper agreement, wages to be paid before Police Magistrate, at Somerset, at the expiration of it.

I request that you will send me instructions how I am to act in this matter; I do not know if I shall be exceeding my duty by acting as shipping master; Mr. Jardine tells me that he was appointed as such. The fisheries here seem in first-rate working order; if I refuse to act as shipping master, I feel that it will capsize the working of the fisheries in these Straits, and lead to the captains of vessels taking natives against their will, which they dare not attempt now. As Mr. Jardine is going down, he will be able to explain this better than I can by letter. I have determined to act as shipping master, doing as little as I can in the matter until I hear from you. I hope my decision in this matter will meet with your approval.

I have carefully taken an inventory of the stores on the Settlement, and Lieutenant Rendell, at my request, placed an officer on the survey of those that were perfectly useless, the report of which I enclose. I did not consider it necessary to survey the buildings, as I understand that you know the state they are in.

I received a letter from Mr. Jardine, requesting me to hold an inquiry into certain charges that have been made against him in the Brisbane papers, which request I have complied with, and enclose proceedings to you.

I also enclose licenses granted by Mr. Jardine to his brother, Mr. Charles Jardine, which you instructed me to get if possible.

Mr. Jardine takes the license of the "Vampire" down with him. As to my instructions relative to Dugald McArthur, master of "Lizzie Jardine," I have made all the inquiries I can in his absence; the evidence he gave at the inquiries held by Mr. Jardine, on the occasion of his getting the cutter aground between Halfway and Somerset, is most contradictory; his great fault seems to be too great a love for drink; if I can keep him from it, I shall not dismiss him until I can get another master, or you appoint one. Coxswain Brown is unfit for duty with a bad leg, and is likely to be so for some time. In the present unsettled state of the natives, I think it would be unwise of me to go away in the cutter, in which case I should have to leave the Settlement in charge of one of the men.

The horses, 19 in number, are very old and poor from want of feed, which is very scarce at present, especially the two draught horses, one of which has his stifle put out. There are about 100 head of quiet cattle about the place, the rest run as far as 60 miles from the Settlement. I cannot do anything in the way of mustering until the horses improve. I have killed a small steer (the best I could find) for beef, it was hardly fit for food.

The Settlement will be without meat until you send us some sheep or preserved meat, if possible I will purchase some of the latter from a passing vessel.

I would call to your notice that there is only one boat belonging to the Settlement, and it cannot be launched below half-tide; I would suggest that the Settlement be supplied with a dingy.

The arms belonging to the Settlement, with the exception of two Snider's and five breech-loading fowling pieces, are very primitive; in fact, I might say, that all arms not suited for waterproof ammunition are useless, or very dangerous in this climate. I would suggest that the Settlement be supplied with at least 12 Snider carbines and 10 Adams' breech-loading pistols. The water police of the Settlement have laid a complaint before me about their rations, and request that they may be placed on the navy scale of rations; I do not consider the navy scale would be suitable, but have drawn up a scale, which I enclose for your approval, that I think would be a great boon to the men, the present station scale of rations is certainly not adapted.

I have, &c.,
C. E. BEDDOME,
Police Magistrate.

To The Honorable The Colonial Secretary, Brisbane.

Evidence taken before Mr. C. E. Beddome, Police Magistrate, Somerset, Cape York, 10th November, 1873.

COXSWAIN EDMONDS BROWN sworn and examined.

1. *By Mr. Beddome*: Have you any complaints to make against Mr. Jardine? None.
2. Have you ever been employed in any boats pearl-shelling? Never whilst in Government employ, except during my leave, when I was working on my own account.
3. Have the Government boats ever been employed in pearl-shelling? No.
4. Is this the license the "Vampire" has been sailing under [*license produced*]? Yes; and she was used as a police boat, and flew the blue ensign.
5. Do you certify that the log of the "Vampire," signed by you, is correct? Yes, as in the book.

EDMONDS BROWN,
Coxswain Water Police.

FREDERICK DWYER, Water Police, sworn and examined.

1. *By Mr. Beddome*: Have you any complaints to make against Mr. Jardine? None.
2. Have you ever been employed in any boats pearl-shelling? No.
3. Have the Government boats ever been employed in pearl-shelling? No.
4. Is this the license the "Vampire" has been sailing under [*license produced*]? Yes.
5. Do you certify that the log of the "Vampire," signed by you, is correct? Yes.

FREDERICK DWYER,
Water Police.

HUMPHREY

HUMPHREY DAVEY MILLS, Water Police, sworn and examined.

1. *By Mr. Beddome:* Have you any complaints to make against Mr. Jardine? None.
2. Have you ever been employed in any boats pearl-shelling? No.
3. Have the Government boats ever been employed in pearl-shelling? Never, to my knowledge.

H. DAVEY MILLS.

JOHN MOORMAN, Water Police, sworn and examined.

1. *By Mr. Beddome:* Have you any complaints to make against Mr. Jardine? None.
2. Have you ever been employed in any boats pearl-shelling? No.
3. Have the Government boats ever been employed in pearl-shelling? Not to my knowledge.

JOHN MOORMAN,
Water Police.

C. E. BEDDOME, Police Magistrate.
FREDK. J. RENDELL, Lieutenant Commanding H.M.S. "Beagle."

SEPARATE APPENDIX C.

No. 1.

LICENSE.

THIS is to certify, that in pursuance of an Act of the Governor and Council passed in the ninth year of the reign of Her Majesty Queen Victoria, intituled "*An Act to Provide for the General Regulation of the Customs in New South Wales*," Frank Lascelles Jardine, of Somerset, in the Colony of Queensland, owner of the boat "Vampire," of the following dimensions,—length, 34 feet; breadth, 10 feet; clinker built, with a sharp stem; two masts; having, together with two sureties, entered into a bond, under date September 25th, 1872, as required by the said Act, the said boat called the "Vampire" is hereby duly licensed to be employed to trade, and in the conveyance of goods and passengers on the coast of Queensland.

A. H. PALMER,
Colonial Secretary, Queensland.

Somerset, September 25th, 1872.

SEPARATE APPENDIX D.

PAPERS HANDED TO THE BOARD BY MR. J. T. COCKERILL, AND FORWARDED TO THE HONORABLE A. H. PALMER, WHOSE REMARKS THEREON WILL BE FOUND IN ITALICS, IN BRACKETS.

The Honorable Colonial Secretary says in his letter to the *Courier*, August the 7th,—[*The Colonial Secretary never wrote a letter to the "Courier," but he did furnish the information for a paragraph*]—that he is in possession of a very large amount dishonored notes and cheques [*see Enclosure No.* 1] for provisions supplied from the Government Stores at Cape York, amongst which is one from or belonging to the writer, (myself), for the sum of £4 15s. odd. [*£3 19s. 2d.—see Enclosure No.* 2.] I scarcely need say there is not one word of truth in the assertion concerning myself. As to the other cheques and orders I can readily believe him, but is there no possibility of finding these defaulters, if they ever existed? The whole of the pearl fishers are easily counted, their stations known, also their receiving ships; it is not at all probable these parties could be allowed to rob the Government with impunity; the strangers are easily counted, they are few and far between, and could only want sufficient to reach Cleveland Bay, say 500 miles, unless they wanted the Government to find provisions for their private fishery. I doubt much if Mr. Jardine would allow this without security, and take very doubtful cheques to the extent the Colonial Secretary now states. Should this be out of the jurisdiction of the present Commission the Legislature may probably take it up.

For the guidance of this Committee, and on behalf of the Government and public generally, I beg respectfully that this Commission will allow me to ask the following questions:—

1. Did the honorable Colonial Secretary ever receive the large amount of cheques and orders as stated in the *Courier*? If so, would the Colonial Secretary kindly furnish your Committee with the following information to enable your Royal Commission to arrive at a just decision in this matter?
2. On the receipt of the first parcel of these worthless orders and cheques, did he inform Mr. Jardine of the fact by letter, stating that he (Mr. Jardine) would be held accountable in future, and called upon to pay the amount out of his own pocket? [*No.—See Enclosure No.* 3.]
3. If so, did he (the Colonial Secretary) receive another batch, and order another letter to be sent to Mr. Jardine demanding his cheque for the amount claimed on behalf of the Government? [*No.—See Enclosure No.* 4.]
4. If so, did the Colonial Secretary wait for nearly one year without getting either answer or cheque, and send another order more, calling his attention, and demanding immediate payment, and receive an evasive answer, but no cheque? [*No.*]
5. Lastly, gave up all further correspondence in this matter? [*No.—See Enclosure No.* 5.]

The above questions are part of a conversation I had with Mr. Jardine, whether true or false remains to be proven.

I have, &c.,
J. T. COCKERILL.

CONDEMNATION OF GOVERNMENT STORES AT THE FREE PORT AND HARBOR OF REFUGE, CAPE YORK. PRESENTED BY J. T. COCKERILL, LATE MASTER OF THE "NATURALIST" SCHOONER, CAPE YORK, TO THE OFFICERS OF THE ROYAL COMMISSION, BRISBANE, DECEMBER 22, 1873.

The Colonial Secretary says in his letter to the *Courier*, August 7th, on account of the quantity of condemned stores at Cape York, the charges for provisions are so high. Having been Commissariat Storekeeper at Hong Kong for some years I well know the duties of that office;—whenever stores were condemned I had to arrange them; give all information to the officers surveying after they were condemned; I had to witness their sale or destruction, and sign vouchers how they were destroyed—whether by sale, fire, or water—and at once hand them over to my superior officer; during the whole time, four years, this was never omitted by me. As the Government Royal Commission now sitting invite any information on the subject, I now humbly request they will call upon the proper officers (not known to me) to produce, for their guidance, and to enable them to do justice to the Crown as well as the accused, all the vouchers connected with the destruction of the stores at Somerset, setting forth the date of each condemnation; the quantity of each particular article; if by fire, water, or sale; the officer who condemned the stores, and the voucher from the storekeeper, and such other modes of arriving at the truth as they may think fit.

J. T. COCKERILL,
Late Master of the "Naturalist."

P.S.—

P.S.—To include the Government boat condemned in February, 1871, by the officer of H.M. man-of-war lying at Somerset at the time. State if sold, destroyed, or repaired in February, 1872; the vouchers of condemnation, and mode of destruction, if any.

J. T. COCKERILL.

[*Enclosure No.* 1.]

LIST OF DISHONORED CHEQUES AND ORDERS.

		£	s.	d.
1871.				
1 October	John Delargy ...	11	6	3
1870.				
14 December ...	W. Whaite ...	4	13	10
1872.				
25 September ...	T. Turpin	2	13	6
11 December ...	J. O. Hogg	15	0	0
31 December ...	D. D. Daly	2	7	6
21 October ...	G. G. MacLachlan ...	20	0	0
28 December ...	D. D. Daly	8	2	0
1873.				
13 January	G. G. MacLachlan	10	0	0
21 March	F. Dwyer ...	3	18	6
1872.				
1 January	James T. Cockerill ...	3	19	2
		£82	0	9

[*Enclosure No.* 2.]

Somerset, Port Albany,
January 1st, 1872.

Mr. J. T. Cockerill, Brisbane.

Please pay the Honorable the Treasurer, or bearer, the sum of three pounds nineteen shillings and two pence sterling.

£3 19s. 2d.

JAMES F. COCKERILL.

Brisbane, 11th March, 1872.

Herewith.

Order—James Cockerill.

For three pounds nineteen shillings and two pence on account Harbor of Refuge, Somerset, being for sale of stores.

£3 19s. 2d.

SIDNEY BRIGGS TERRY,
Chief Clerk.

To the Under Secretary, Treasury.

Order returned, Mr. Cockerill having left Brisbane.

E. B. C.

[*Enclosure No.* 3.]

EXTRACT FROM LETTER, 27TH JANUARY, 1872, No. D-72-41, FROM THE UNDER COLONIAL SECRETARY TO THE POLICE MAGISTRATE, SOMERSET.

* * * I take this opportunity of acquainting you that it is not desirable to dispose of stores, &c., to the masters of ships passing, except for cash.

The orders they draw upon their owners, or agents, are frequently dishonored, and there is always great difficulty in obtaining payment.

I enclose you a notice of dishonored order of £4 13s. 10d., drawn by Wm. Whaite, on James Montgomery, Sydney. * * *

[*Enclosure No.* 4.]

D-73-200.

Colonial Secretary's Office,
Brisbane, 28th April, 1873.

SIR,

Adverting to a former communication respecting the sale of stores to the masters of ships and others, I have again to impress upon you that in the event of its being necessary to part with any portion of the supplies forwarded for the use of the establishment at Somerset, payment must only be made in cash, or in an equivalent in articles required, or likely to be serviceable to the settlement, taken in exchange.

The orders drawn by masters of ships on their owners, or otherwise, are invariably dishonored, and there is no means of recovering the amount.

I have, &c.,
H. H. MASSIE.

The Police Magistrate, Somerset.

[*Enclosure No.* 5.]

D-73-350.

Colonial Secretary's Office,
Brisbane, 7th July, 1873.

F. Dwyer, Bank N. S. Wales, £3 18s 6d. No account.
W. Blount, Bank N. S. Wales, £3 9s. 9d. No account.

SIR,

Adverting to your letter of 31st March, accompanying the Government Store cash account for the quarter ended on that date, with a remittance in cheques, orders, and cash of £132 16s., in payment of goods sold, I have the honor to inform you that the cheques enumerated in the margin have been presented and dishonored.

No return has as yet been received of the cheques and orders forwarded to parts beyond the colony for collection.

I have, &c.,
H. H. MASSIE.

The Police Magistrate, Somerset.

[Enclosure

[*Enclosure No. 6.*]

D-73-511.

Colonial Secretary's Office,
Brisbane, 16th October, 1873.

Sir,

With reference to the remittance of £132 16s., on account of sales of Government Stores, according to the statement forwarded under cover of your letter of 31st March last, I have the honor to enclose for your information copy of a letter received from the Colonial Treasury, under date 15th September last, whereby you will perceive that of the above remittance cheques and orders to the amount of £59 8s. have been dishonored on presentation; and your attention is directed to the necessity of the instructions issued on previous occasions being complied with, relating to the mode of payment of stores supplied to ships in want of provisions, which, whenever practicable, is to be by way of barter or exchange of commodities.

I have, &c.,
H. H. MASSIE.

The Police Magistrate, Somerset.

[*Enclosure No. 7.*]

Colonial Secretary's Office,
7th January, 1874.

Memo.—A survey in due form has always been made on damaged or useless stores before they are condemned or destroyed, and a list of the articles condemned, duly certified, is forwarded by the first opportunity to the Colonial Secretary.

Advantage has generally been taken of the visit of one of H.M.'s ships to the station, to have the survey made by one or more of the officers.

The last survey was made by Sub-Lieutenant Underwood of H.M.S. "Beagle," in the form annexed.

H. H. MASSIE.

[*Enclosure No. 8.*]

List of Articles Condemned at Somerset, 8th day of November, 1873.

Article	No.	Article	No.
Basins, iron	4	Smith, black, tools	1 set
Bedsteads, iron	1	Tomahawks	6
Buckets, galvanised	3	Braces	1
Chamber pots	2	Knives, drawing	1
Kettles, tin mess	6	Barrels flour	4
Kettles, iron tea	1	Bench, armourers'	1
Kids, mess, tin, large	5	Blocks, single	2
Kids, mess, tin, small	0	Cans, oil, tin	2
Lamps, hand, oil	9	Diamonds, glaziers'	2
Lamps, moderator	1	Drills, steel boring	1
Lantern, small barrack	1	Drills, iron boring	1
Ovens, camp	1	Feeders, oil tin	1
Pails, slop tin	1	Locks, pad	1
Pans, dust tin	1	Mallets, masons'	2
Pans, bed	2	Pots, quart, tin	4
Plates, tin	10	Shovels	1
Pots, 3-leg iron	1	Spades	1
Pots, iron enamel	1	Stoves, iron	1
Spoons, iron	9	Tanks, zinc	9
Axes, broad	1	Tape line	1
Axes, falling	1	Wheelbarrow, iron	1
Bits, for brace	21	Clocks, small	1
Bradawls	2	Breast relievers	1
Chisels, firmer	3	Rakes, garden	1
Gimlets	4	Handcuffs	4
Forge, smiths'	1	Shower bath	1
Mallets	1	Hip bath	1
Beading plane	1	Combs, curry	2
Rasps, wood	2	Combs, mane	1
Rule, 2-foot	1	Mustard, lbs	6
Saws, cross cut	1		

We have made a careful survey of the above stores, the property of the Queensland Government, at Somerset, and find them perfectly useless, and condemn them to be thrown away.

Given under our hands this day.

C. E. BEDDOME,
Police Magistrate.
P. C. UNDERWOOD,
Sub-Lieut. H.M.S. "Beagle."

Somerset, 8th November, 1873.

Price 1s.]

By Authority: James C. Beal, Government Printer, William street, Brisbane.

www.ingramcontent.com/pod-product-compliance
Lightning Source LLC
Chambersburg PA
CBHW021550270326
41930CB00008B/1453

9783744646864